Fruitful Vine And Olive Shoots

Fruitful Vine

AND

Olive Shoots

Uche Ezechim

XULON PRESS

Xulon Press
2301 Lucien Way #415
Maitland, FL 32751
407.339.4217
www.xulonpress.com

Unless otherwise indicated, Scripture quotations taken from the King
James Version (KJV) – *public domain.*

Printed in the United States of America.

ISBN-13: 978-1-6305-0865-4

All Trade Orders to:
Uche Ezechim
Phone Number: +1905 232 2457
+1647 272 1968
E-mail: fruitfulrehoboth@gmail.com

Author's Bio

The author holds a Bachelor of Arts degree in English Language/ Literature from Abia State University Uturu Nigeria, as well as a post graduate degree in Education from York University, Toronto Canada. She is an experienced educator with extraordinary passion to positively impact the Mountain of Education for the Lord.

Uche Ezechim, as an ambassador of Jesus Christ, loves the Lord deeply and is completely sold out to advance the work of His Kingdom. A nurturing shepherd, worship leader, profound teacher of the Word of God, a thinker, a writer, fervent intercessor, a virtuous woman, and a joyful mother of Godly seeds. She is one of the American Continental Coordinators of Wailing Women Worldwide with strong prophetic and administrative gifts. The author is a trailblazer with great apostolic unction and grace; who disciples and raises leaders across the nations. Uche and her husband Engr. Ezekiel Ezechim are Founders of Grace Apostolic Ministries; an Interdenominational Missionary Intercessory Outreach within Canada and beyond.

DEDICATION

To the King Eternal, Immortal, Invisible, the only wise God, be glory and honour, forever and ever Amen!

To His Excellency, the Heavenly Governor, the Holy Spirit, who is the source of all truth and life.

To all Christian couples who are waiting on God's miraculous intervention for their promised child or children.

To Family Prayer Network, whose mandate is to rescue, recover, reconcile, rebuild, reposition and restore families to the divine purposes of God.

To all the miracle sons and daughters born through effectual, fervent prayer.

TABLE OF CONTENTS

ACKNOWLEDGMENT

I sincerely appreciate Our Heavenly Father for inspiring and enabling me to complete this book, you are indeed faithful. Thank you for sustaining the passion, interest and commitment to get this done. Holy Spirit, my Senior Partner, Teacher, Helper and Advocate, I reverence You for being with me every step of the way.

I deeply appreciate my one and only husband, Pastor Ezekiel Ezechim, with whom I had these experiences. I love you, honey.

There could have been no *Fruitful Vine and Olive Shoots* book without Glory, Covenant and Jachimike. I am eternally grateful to God the Creator for bringing these Godly Seeds into my life. You all are a great inspiration to me.

I acknowledge my friends and all those who committed to pray consistently for me.

I thank God Almighty for Dr. Steve Ogan, who edited and typeset this book. He is the springboard who helped me to gather the momentum to finish this book.

I would also like to express my gratitude to the Salem Author Services editorial team, and the publisher for a job well done. Shalom!

Uche Ezechim
Ontario Certified Teacher (OCT)

Preface

According to the World Health Organization, every year an estimated 40-50 million abortions are done corresponding to approximately 125,000 abortions per day. Is it then possible that there are still couples who desperately desire to have children? Considering the medical advancement and inventions of treating infertility in today's world, do people still have faith and trust in God for supernatural conception? The answers to these questions and more are hidden in this little treasure you are holding in your hands.

Fruitful Vine and Olive Shoots is a manifestation of the divine inspiration I received in my pregnancies, childbirth and post-natal experiences. Through the processes it became very clear that our experiences were not just for us. We were helped in order to help someone, empowered in order to empower someone, delivered to deliver someone, comforted to comfort someone, blessed in order to ultimately be a blessing to people.

The principle you are about to discover in this book defies all medical, spiritual and hereditary factors that cause infertility.

My target audience includes:

- Husbands and wives desperately waiting and trusting God Almighty for conception and miracle babies.
- Parents and grandparents standing in the gap for their married children for the fruit of the womb and safe delivery.
- Counsellors and prayer intercessors who daily counsel and stand in the gap for friends seeking for children.
- Those who know someone whose case needs only divine intervention and mercy to conceive and bear children.
- Those who need additional knowledge on infertility or delay in childbirth.

My husband and I have a remarkable testimony in the area of supernatural childbirth. We are passionate about extending the same opportunity to all and sundry. We pray compassionately and minister with great faith to those who have a similar need, and by the grace of God the results we get are intriguing. Infertility, even of many years, is being broken; children are being miraculously birthed as a heritage of the Lord and His reward to couples.

I conceived the idea to write this book many years ago. I have patiently withheld sharing the full testimony of the birth of our three miracle children until now as friends, family and brethren only know the tip of the iceberg of the story. This book contains the complete amazing praise report that will inspire anyone to eternally fear and reverence the Sovereign Lord.

I encourage every reader to be very sensitive to every single detail, apply the principles in this book to your life situation, study every scripture and believe every Word of God and prophetic declaration. But above all, expect a miracle, for there shall be a performance of those things which are spoken to you by the Lord. Amen.

FOREWORD

I knew Pastor (Mrs.) Uche and her husband, Engr. Pastor Ezekiel Ezechim when they were in Port Harcourt, Nigeria when I was based in Cross Rivers State. We prayed together for the fruit of the womb and for growth in their ministry. God spoke to them about their relocation to Canada and that they would bear their children. However, it did not make great sense; neither did it seem real, judging by what was on the ground then. Nevertheless, today I am privileged to write the foreword of a book where the testimony of the fulfilled Word of God is documented. I am very refreshed and would want you to share in this refreshing.

I visited them in Canada four times to see and touch the evidence of God's faithfulness and His mercies. The testimonies in this book are real and only point to the fact that God's Word is forever settled in Heaven as recorded in Psalm 119: 89. God's promises in Christ Jesus are yea and Amen (2 Cor. 1:20) and if God has spoken, He will hasten His word to perform it (Jer. 1:12).

Another important aspect of this story is the personal drive of the author and her husband to realize what God promised them. Proverbs 12:27 paints a graphic picture of the very reason many people do not receive the promises of God. *"The slothful (lazy) man roasteth not that which he took in hunting."* God is a rewarder of them who "diligently" seek Him (Heb. 11:6). This book teaches us to aggressively and diligently take hold of God's promises to us until they are realized physically.

I therefore strongly recommend this book to everyone who has respect for God and desires a fulfillment of His promises in his or her life. I also recommend it to people who are yet to taste the saving grace and strength of the Lord Jesus Christ. May this small but truthful and powerful book become a doorway to your desired miracle. My prayer also is that this book will richly bless all its readers and whoever will hear the testimonies through you, the reader. Amen.

Dr. Ikechukwu Gregory Ugwu
Altar of Favor, Warri, Nigeria

FOREWORD

U che Ezechim, the author of *The Fruitful Vine and Olive Shoots,* is a beloved Sister and friend, a lover of God and His Word, a passionate intercessor, a counsellor and a worshipper. She is one of the American Continental Coordinators of the Wailing Women Worldwide.

This book is timely, and its content can be summed up in the words of 2nd Corinthians 1:3-4:

"Blessed be God, even the Father of our Lord Jesus Christ, the Father of mercies, and the God of all comfort; Who comforteth us in all our tribulation, that we may be able to comfort them which are in any trouble, by the comfort wherewith we ourselves are comforted of God."

It is a down-to-earth documentation of the personal experience of Uche and her dear husband Ezekiel in their journey from infertility to being joyful parents of three children!

Having gone through the ordeal, Uche is better able, from experiential knowledge, to identify with the pains and distress of couples going through the same challenge of infertility.

Her testimony attests to the practical reality of God's divine power and ability to intervene in the affairs of men. It tells of wholehearted dependence on God, faith in His Word, a Kingdom lifestyle and a life of fervent prayer with fasting.

She addresses the medical, emotional and spiritual aspects of the problem and proffers the solution that worked for her to seekers. The book is easy to read and understand and is highly recommended for couples who desire to have children of their own.

May the Lord use the content of the book to break the yoke of barrenness and bring joy and gladness to homes.

Dr. Mrs. Olaide Okafor
Wailing Women Worldwide.

I Know The Author

The Servant Leader

I have known Uche Ezechim for five years as she has been the lead National Coordinator of Wailing Women Worldwide, Canada. During my first year in Wailing Women Worldwide Canada,

though I had not met her in person Uche would call me always to know how I was doing. She would listen, answer my questions, and after an hour or more, she would pray for me.

It was only later when I got to know more about her that I understood the value of those calls. I learned that Uche was not only the leader of WWW Canada but a pastor in a church, a mother to three young children, a wife, a counsellor and a teacher. Yet,

when I ask her if she is available to talk, she makes time. This spirit of servant leadership is invariably evident in all areas I know Uche in, for I have seen her gladly give her time, money and strength to others when needed. I'm grateful for the opportunity to give honour to this true woman of God. Paul told the Corinthians to follow his example as he imitates Christ. I thank my God that He has given me and many others an example, a co-worker and sister in Christ, to follow.

Julie Russell
Secondary School Educator
British Columbia, Canada

Woman Of Faith

T o say Uche is a woman of faith is an understatement. Her faith in God is evident in every area of her life and has a way of influencing those around her. This comes out of the close rela-

tionship she has developed with the Lord; one she continues to nurture on a regular basis. This book will challenge the faith of its readers. Your faith will leap as you read. You will run in your faith if you were walking, and you will fly if you were running. Her story will inspire the reader's faith and will encourage a closer relationship with God. The anointing on this book will

transform your life for good.

Olive Tetteh-Hervie,
Sales Operations Business Partner Specialist,
British Columbia, Canada

U che is a woman of faith; such that transcends human reasoning or imagination and that quality attracted me to her and her family. She is a child of God who is completely sold out to her calling and is passionate about whatever course she believes in. This is evident in her life and ministry.

Rita Duyile,
Child & Youth Worker,
Caledon, Ontario, Canada

U che is a woman of faith, one who truly knows her God and can testify that He never fails. She is an intercessor and is passionate about fulfilling her God-given destiny on earth. She always stands for what she believes in, even when no one is standing with her. I consider her an encourager, a mentor and a friend. A woman who fears the Lord deserves to be praised.

Rose Mwinyi,
Business Owner,
Pickering Ontario, Canada.

Lover Of God

I have known the author since the year I joined the Wailing Women Worldwide, Canada. What struck me about Pastor Mrs.

Uche Ezechim is her love and passion for God and His work. During my orientation, she taught and explained the vision of the Wailing Women and also talked with conviction about God's power and authority. She would always say *"I will bless the Lord at all times, His praise shall continually be in my mouth."* She always repeats this same phrase in any situation. After reading the short summary of her book, I now understand why God chose her as an instrument carved for Himself. Waiting for God's time is not an easy task, especially in African culture where you are pressurized from all angles. I hope their testimony will be a blessing to all who read it.

Evangelist Mabel Sampson,
Office Manager/Pastor,
Ottawa, Canada.

True Worshipper

S o much can be said in praise of this chosen, mighty vessel of God, with whom I have had the distinct privilege of linking arms and uniting hearts in worship and intercession over the last five years. Throughout our journey, I have discovered that the hidden

'SECRET' to her effectiveness and usefulness to God, is that she is a 'true worshipper' of God. Regardless of the circumstances, in the midst of storms, valleys, mountaintops, trials and in the triumphs, her worship purely reflects His WORTH-ship, as 'DEEP calls out to DEEP'. All of her gifts, anointing, and fruitful works of service find their source and expression from her worship. What an inspiration, worthy of imitation! The scripture instructs us to *'Imitate those who through faith and patience inherit what has been promised'* (Hebrews 6:12).

Esther Knights

Director, Zion House of Prayer, Montreal,
Missions Base of Streams of Zion Restoration
Ministries, Canada.
www.streamsofzion.org

INTRODUCTION

A ccording to Dr. Copperman, *"It's harder to get pregnant than you think."* This may sound like music to the ears of singles who are nowhere ready to have children. However, the reality of infertility is daunting, stressful and extremely life-interrupting.

Alan B. Copperman, M.D., Director of the division of Reproductive Endocrinology and infertility at Mount Sinai Hospital and medical director of *Reproductive Medicine Associates of New York,* said that, *"Not all eggs are normal, not all normal eggs implant. There's actually only about a 15 to 20 percent chance in any given month that a couple will conceive."*

Research shows that in the U.S., 6.7 million women between the ages of fifteen and forty-four have an impaired ability to get pregnant or carry a baby to term. According to the Center for Disease Control (CDC), about 6% of married women fifteen to forty-four years of age are unable to get pregnant after one year of trying.

Obviously, infertility could be a medical condition that can affect the way you feel about yourself, your relationship with your spouse and your overall perspective on living. It can also be particularly stressful in that; it creates a great deal of uncertainty and emotional upheaval in a couple's day-to-day world. You become too familiar with stress when struggling with infertility.

This book recommends ways to reduce your anxiety, remain hopeful and live your life to the fullest according to the plan of God. Irrespective of the cause of infertility, do not lose hope and faith in the Sovereign, all-powerful, Great Physician and Great Deliverer. You will be a living proof that the power to conceive and bring forth children belongs to God Almighty alone.

The principles you are about to discover in this book surpass all medical, spiritual, hereditary and psychological factors of primary or secondary infertility.

In many countries, infertility refers to a couple who has failed to conceive after 12 months of regular sexual intercourse without the use of contraception. Infertility can also refer to the biological inability of an individual to contribute to conception, or to a female who cannot carry a pregnancy to full term.

Secondary infertility refers to couples who have been able to get pregnant at least once, but now is unable. (Source–Medical News Today, Christian Nordqvist, reviewed by Debra Rose Wilson, Ph.D., MSN, RN, IBCLC, AHN-BC, CHT).

Risks, Factors and Causes Of Infertility

In medicine, a risk factor is something that raises the risk of developing a condition, disease or symptom.

1. **Age–**A woman's fertility starts to drop after she is about thirty-two years old. A fifty-year-old man is usually less fertile than a man in his twenties (male fertility progressively drops after the age of forty).
2. **Smoking–**Smoking significantly increases the risk of infertility in both men and women. Smoking may also undermine the effects of fertility treatment. Even a pregnant woman who smokes has a greater risk of miscarriage.
3. **Alcohol Consumption–**a woman's pregnancy can be seriously affected by any amount of alcohol consumption. Alcohol abuse may lower male fertility. Moderate alcohol consumption has not been shown to lower fertility in most

men but is thought to lower fertility in men who already have a low sperm count.

4. **Being Obese or Overweight**–In industrialized countries, being overweight or obese, or having a sedentary lifestyle are often found to be the principal causes of female infertility. An overweight man has a higher risk of having abnormal sperm.

5. **Eating Disorders**–Women who are seriously underweight because of an eating disorder may have fertility problems.

6. **Being Vegan**–If you are a strict vegan, you must make sure your intake of iron, folic acid, zinc and vitamin B12 are adequate. Otherwise, your fertility may be affected.

7. **Over-Exercising**–A woman who exercises for more than seven hours each week may have ovulation problems.

8. **Not exercising** – A sedentary lifestyle is sometimes linked to lack of exercise and it lowers fertility in both men and women.

9. **Sexually Transmitted Infections** (STIs)–Chlamydia can damage the fallopian tubes, as well as making the man's scrotum become inflamed. Some other STIs may also cause infertility.

10. **Exposure to Some Chemicals**–Some pesticides, herbicides, metals (lead) and solvents have led to fertility problems in both men and women.

11. **Mental Stress**–Studies indicate that female ovulation and sperm production may be affected by mental stress. If a partner is stressed, it is possible that the frequency of sexual intercourse will be lower, thus resulting in a smaller chance of conception.

Some Medical Causes Of Infertility In Women

There are many possible causes of infertility such as medical, spiritual, hereditary, emotional and psychological, but unfortunately, about one-third of infertility cases have no identified cause.

Ovulation Disorders

Problems with ovulation are the most common cause of infertility in women, experts say. Ovulation is the monthly release of an egg. In some cases, the woman never releases eggs, while in others; the woman does not release eggs during some cycles. Ovulation disorders can be due to:

1. **Premature Ovarian Failure**–The woman's ovaries stop working before the age of 40.
2. **Polycystic Ovary Syndrome (PCOS)**–The woman's ovaries function abnormally. She also has abnormally high levels of androgen. About 5% to 10% of women of reproductive age are affected to some degree by this condition. It is also called Stein-Leventhal syndrome.
3. **Hyperprolactinemia**–If prolactin levels are high and the woman is not pregnant or breastfeeding, this may affect ovulation and fertility.
4. **Poor Egg Quality**–Eggs that are damaged or develop genetic abnormalities cannot sustain a pregnancy. The older a woman is, the higher the risk.
5. **Other Factors**–Other factors that may contribute to infertility include: overactive thyroid gland or underactive thyroid gland and some chronic conditions, such as AIDS or Cancer.

Problems In The Uterus Or Fallopian Tubes

The egg travels from the ovary to the uterus (womb), where the fertilized egg grows. If there is something wrong in the uterus or the fallopian tubes, the woman may not be able to conceive naturally. This may be due to:

1. **Surgery**–Pelvic surgery can sometimes cause scarring or damage to the fallopian tubes. Cervical surgery can sometimes cause scarring or shortening of the cervix. The cervix is the neck of the uterus.

2. **Submucosal Fibroids**–These are benign or non-cancerous tumors found in the muscular wall of the uterus that occurs in 30% to 40% of women of childbearing age. They may interfere with implantation and block the fallopian tube, preventing sperm from fertilizing the egg. Large submucosal uterine fibroids may make the uterus cavity bigger, increasing the distance the sperm has to travel.

3. **Endometriosis**–Cells that are normally found within the lining of the uterus that start growing elsewhere in the body.

4. **Previous Sterilization Treatment**–If a woman chose to have her fallopian tubes blocked, it is possible to reverse this process, but the chances of becoming fertile again are not high.

5. **Medications**–Some drugs can affect the fertility of a woman, such drugs include:
    1. **NSAIDs** (Non-Steroidal Anti-Inflammatory Drugs):– Women who take aspirin or ibuprofen long-term may find it hard to conceive.
    2. **Chemotherapy**:–Some medications used in chemotherapy can result in ovarian failure. In some cases, this side effect of chemotherapy may be permanent.

3. **Radiotherapy**–If radiation therapy was aimed near the woman's reproductive organs there is a higher risk of fertility problems.
4. **Illegal Drugs** -Some women who take marijuana or cocaine may have fertility problems.

Some Causes Of Infertility In Men

Abnormal Semen: This is responsible for about 75% of all cases of male infertility. Unfortunately, doctors never find out why. The following semen problems are possible:

1. **Low Sperm Count** (Low Concentration): The man ejaculates a lesser amount of sperm compared to other men. Sperm concentration should be about 20 million sperm per millilitre of semen. A count that is under 10 million is a low sperm concentration (subfertility).
2. **No Sperm**: When the man ejaculates without any sperm in the semen.
3. **Low Sperm Motility**: The sperm cannot "swim" as well as it should.
4. **Abnormal Sperm**–The sperm has an unusual shape, making it more difficult to move and fertilize an egg. Sperm must be shaped correctly and able to travel rapidly and accurately towards the egg. If the sperm's morphology (structure) and motility (movement) are wrong, it is less likely the egg would be fertilized. Testicular infection, Testicular cancer, and Testicular surgery may cause abnormal semen.
5. **Overheating the Testicles**–Frequent saunas, hot tubs, very hot baths, or working in extremely hot environments can raise the temperature of the testicles. Tight clothing may have the same effect on some people.

6. **Ejaculation Disorders**: Men with retrograde ejaculation, ejaculate semen into the bladder. If the ejaculatory ducts are blocked or obstructed, the man may have a problem ejaculating appropriately.

7. **Varicocele**: This is a varicose vein in the scrotum that may cause the sperm to overheat.

8. **Undescended Testicle**: One testicle (or both) fails to descend from the abdomen into the scrotum during fetal development. Sperm production is affected because the testicle is not in the scrotum and is at a higher temperature. Healthy sperm need to exist in a slightly lower-than-body temperature environment. That is why they are in the scrotum and not inside the body.

9. **Hypogonadism**–Testosterone deficiency can result in a disorder of the testicles.

10. **Genetic Abnormality**: Every man should have an X and a Y chromosome. If he has two X chromosomes and one Y chromosome (Klinefelter's syndrome), there will be an abnormal development of the testicles, low testosterone, and a low sperm count (sometimes no sperm at all).

11. **Mumps**: This viral infection usually affects young children. However, if it occurs after puberty, inflammation of the testicles may affect sperm production.

12. **Hypospadias**: This is when the urethral opening is at the underside of the penis, instead of its tip. This abnormality is usually surgically corrected when the male is a baby. If it is not, the sperm may find it harder to get to the female cervix. Hypospadias occurs in about 1 in every 500 newborn boys.

13. **Cystic Fibrosis**–Cystic fibrosis is a chronic disease that affects organs such as the liver, lungs, pancreas and intestines. It disrupts the body's salt balance, leaving too little salt and water on the outside of cells and cause the thin layer of mucus that usually keeps the lungs free of germs

to become thick and sticky. This mucus is difficult to cough out and it clogs the lungs and airways, leading to infections and damaged lungs. Males with cystic fibrosis commonly have a missing or obstructed vas deferens (tube connecting the testes to the urethra; it carries sperm from the epididymis to the ejaculatory duct and the urethra).

14. **Radiotherapy**: Radiation therapy can impair sperm production. The severity usually depends on how near to the testicles the radiation was aimed.

15. **Diseases**: The following diseases and conditions are sometimes linked to low fertility in males: anemia, Cushing's syndrome, diabetes and thyroid disease.

16. **Illegal Drugs**–Consumption of marijuana and cocaine can lower a man's sperm count.

The Pain Of Infertility

No one ever plans for infertility; you just realize that you are infertile when you are ready to have children. Most people don't know that infertility hurts silently. It is not the loud, screaming kind of pain. It's long, slow and quiet. It is a labour of the soul that occurs when you throw another negative pregnancy test in the trash can and sit behind your bathroom door and cry.

It hurts when your period is late for a few days and you quickly go to your doctor, request a pregnancy test, and the result turns out to be negative.

What is more painful than when you lay in your bed at night and your husband holds you while you gaze into the darkness, and silent tears fall to your pillow?

Labour of the soul is when you sit at a baby shower and hear all the "aww" over every little tiny gift and wonder if you will ever have an opportunity to open your gift.

Then you look at your stomach, put your hand over it and pray
for life to grow, and imagine what it would look like to be pregnant

It hurts when people come up to you and say, "Hey! Isn't it
about time you two started having kids?" You give a big, fake smile
to hide your pain.

When you see teenagers pushing strollers past your house,
when a minivan full of children opens its doors, when a friend
says they had another "unplanned" pregnancy, and you wonder:
"Why is this so easy for everyone else except us?

Or when people make it seem as though God has singled you
out for punishment, by shutting your womb.

I know these pains and feelings because I went through them.
I thought it would be so easy for us to conceive on the first try, but
it wasn't. It took ten years before I became pregnant.

Where Is God When You Can't Get Pregnant?

He is right there with you.

- He is near you during the sleepless nights.
- He sees every secret tear that falls from your eyes.
- He holds your hand when your friend "accidentally" gets pregnant.
- He comforts you as you hold someone else's newborn.

In the midst of seemingly dark and lonely moments, He is
always there to guide, shape, mold, woo, and call you into a deeper,
and more loving relationship with Him.

God shall come through for you, just keep trusting and loving
Him deeper. He shall decorate and beautify you, more than you
can ever imagine. The fruits of a heart without Christ are bitterness,
resentment, anger, jealousy, envy, depression, anxiety, obsession,
grief, intolerance, self-pity, frustration and guilt.

Infertility can either devastate a person or cause the person to triumph over it, depending on one's position of faith in Jesus Christ. It is possible to conquer the pain of infertility by allowing Christ to deal with the negative emotions, reactions and attitudes associated with it. The product of a heart deeply rooted in Christ Jesus will bear the fruits of thankfulness, perseverance, peace, contentment, trust, joy, patience, belief, confidence, courage and freedom.

The Bible assures us that we have authority to *overcome* the power of the enemy (Luke 10:19), that His brilliant light cannot be *overcome* by darkness (John 1:5). And that he who believes that Jesus is the Son of God, has victoriously *overcome* the world (1 John 5:5). Jesus gave us the gift of salvation so that in Him, we can have peace in this world of trouble. Jesus said, "I have overcome the world" (John 16:3). You may not physically overcome infertility, but you shall not carry the burden alone if you are in Christ.

The Bible says, *"Cast your burdens onto Him."* Like the mute son's father, ask Jesus to help you *overcome* your unbelief (Mark 9:24). Bring your unbelief, your burdens, and your darkness to the feet of Jesus. By His power, you can overcome the darkness of infertility.

Let your quest to have children drive you into the Lord's arms, as it is difficult to walk the dark and lonely road of infertility in true confidence. I assure you that when you run to God, you will know more about Him, as well as who you are *in* Him.

Chapter 1
GOD'S ETERNAL PURPOSE

G od created man in His image and likeness; that is, in holiness and righteousness. Sin found its way into man when Adam and Eve disobeyed God in the Garden of Eden. God created man primarily for His pleasure, companionship, communion and fellowship.

Revelation 4:11 says:

> Thou *art worthy, O Lord, to receive glory and*
> *honour and power: for thou hast created all things,*
> *and for thy pleasure they are and were created.*

After God created man, He took a second look at him and confirmed, *"It is very good." (Genesis 1: 31)*. For man to accomplish procreation, God Almighty proclaimed a unique blessing of multiplication on him, gave him dominion over and above every other thing He created. *"Be fruitful,* and *multiply. Fill the earth and replenish it…" (Genesis 1: 28)*.

The Fall Of Man

A number of persons find themselves making wrong choices, disobeying God's command and living for self-gratification.

However, thank God, *"For the grace of God has appeared, that offers salvation to all people."* (Titus 2:11).

Our churches today are filled with people who hold to a dead faith that cannot save (James 2:17, 20, 26). Paul wrote to the church at Corinth to test or examine themselves, to see if they were truly in the faith (2 Cor. 13:5). If faith was important in Paul's days, how much more important is it for the church today to test her faith?

Where do we start? What are the criteria for determining true faith and empty faith? What are the distinguishing marks of a genuine saving faith? Surprisingly, some popular standards really do not prove the genuineness of one's faith. Before we consider the proof of genuine faith, let's look at some popular tests that neither prove nor disprove the genuineness of one's faith.

Seven Factors That May Not Necessarily Prove Genuine Salvation

1. Visible Morality

There are some people who are naturally good, religious, moral, honest, and forthright, [trustworthy] in their dealings with people. They are grateful, loving, kind and tender-hearted towards others. They even have visible virtues and external morality. The hope of the Pharisees was rested on visible morality; yet, Christ's harshest words were directed at them.

Many people who have good morals know nothing of love for God; they do good works for humanity, but know nothing about service to God, neither do they live for His glory. Though they are honest in their dealings with everyone, they rob God of His praise and honour. They speak contemptuously and reproachfully to God because they do not have any relationship with Him. They are like the rich, young ruler who said in Luke 18: 21 "All these things I have kept from my youth" Their focus is on morals only.

2

2. Intellectual Knowledge

Another factor that can be misleading is intellectual knowledge. People can have an intellectual understanding and knowledge of the truth, yet they are not saved. Knowledge of the truth is not an assurance of true saving faith. People can know all about God the Father, the Son and the Holy Spirit, and can even give details about the life of Christ, but have never received Him as their personal Lord and Saviour.

The writer of Hebrews warns against this factor in Hebrews 6:4-6. There are people in the church who know all about God and understand the scripture, have experienced the ministry of the Holy Spirit or seen Him at work in people's lives, yet they keep rejecting Christ.

Hebrews 10 says that such persons are treading underfoot the Blood of Christ by not accepting the truth, hence they have chosen Satan, the way to hell! A man cannot be saved without having the knowledge of the truth, but he must first accept Jesus as his personal Lord and Saviour and believe that He died and rose again for all men.

3. Religious Involvement

Your religion as a Christian is not necessarily a proof of true faith. According to Paul, there are people who possess an outward form (a mere external appearance) of godliness, but have denied the power of it. Jesus illustrated this in the Parable of the Virgins in Matthew 25. These Virgins waited for the coming of the bridegroom, but as five of them stepped out to get more oil, Jesus came and they missed entering the party hall with Him. The oil is symbolic of the new life, the indwelling of the Holy Spirit; in other words, the virgins were so religious that they refused the Regenerated One.

3

4. Active Ministry

It is possible to have an active and public ministry, without being genuinely saved. Balaam was a prophet, but compromised his ministry because of money (Deut. 23:3-6). Saul of Tarsus (who later became the apostle Paul) thought he was serving God by killing Christians. Judas was a public preacher and one of the twelve disciples of Christ, but became an apostate.

In Matthew 7:22-23, Jesus said,

Many will say to Me in that day, 'Lord, Lord, have we not prophesied in Your name, cast out demons in Your name, and done many wonders in Your name?' And then I will declare to them, 'I never knew you; depart from me, you who practice lawlessness!

Those whom Jesus spoke of were involved in active and public ministry, but Jesus said He never knew them. What a sobering word, indeed!

5. Conviction Of Sin

Conviction of sin is not a proof of salvation. Our world is filled with guilt-ridden people. Many people feel bad when they sin. Felix trembled at the preaching of the apostle Paul, but he never left his idols or turned to God (Acts 24:4-6). The Holy Spirit convicts men of sin, unrighteousness and of judgment, but many persons do not repent genuinely. Some may confess their sins, others may stop the sins they feel guilty about and amend their ways, but shortly they fall out of faith because they did not experience internal regeneration. Conviction of sin is not a conclusive evidence of salvation. Even demons are convicted of their sins and that is why they tremble (James 2:19).

6. The Feeling Of Salvation Assurance

Feeling like you are saved does not guarantee that you are. Someone may say, "Well, I must be a Christian because I feel, or I think I am one." But that is faulty reasoning. If thinking you are a Christian actually makes you one, then no one is saved. Satan wants people to think they are saved. He is deceiving millions of religious people into thinking they are saved even though they are not. To them, God will not condemn them for they feel good about themselves. They are just cool with the assurance of salvation they feel.

7. A Time Of Decision

So often people say, *"Well, I know that I'm a Christian because I remember when I walked to the altar in church, said the salvation prayer, filled out the card and attended foundation class."* Our salvation is not verified by a past moment. Many people have prayed prayers, been baptized in water immersion and are serving in a unit of the church, but they are not truly saved.

What, then, are the marks of genuine salvation? Are there some reliable tests from the Word of God that enable us to know whether our faith is real? There are at least nine Biblical criteria for examining the genuineness of your salvation or faith in Jesus.

Nine Proofs Of Genuine Salvation

1. Love For God

A deep and abiding love for God is one of the supreme evidences of salvation. Romans 8:7 says, *"the carnal mind is enmity [hostility, hatred] against God; for it is not subject to the law of God, nor indeed can be."* Thus, if a man's heart is at enmity with

God there is no basis to assume genuine salvation. Those who are truly saved love God, only sinners resent God, His Sovereignty and are rebellious towards His plan for their life. The regenerated man loves the Lord with all his heart, soul, mind, and strength. He delights in the infinite excellences of God. God is his chief happiness and source of satisfaction; he seeks and thirsts for God like a hungry deer.

We must be careful to distinguish between the love for God that seeks God's glory and self-love that sees God primarily as a means of personal fulfillment and gain. The heart that truly loves God desires to please and glorify God. Jesus taught us that if we love our parents more than we love Him, we are not worthy of Him.

> *He who loves father or mother more than me is not worthy of Me. And he who loves son or daughter more than me is not worthy of Me. And he who does not take his cross and follow me is not worthy of Me. He who finds his life will lose it, and he who loses his life for my sake will find it.*

Matthew 10:37-39

The questions now are: Do you love God? Do you love His nature? Do you love His glory? Do you love His name? Do you love His Kingdom, His holiness and His will? Is your heart filled with love and joy when you sing His praises? Supreme love for God is an evidence of true faith in Christ.

2. Repentance From Sin

We show our genuine love for God by our hatred for sin. If we truly love someone, their best interests and their well-being would be our greatest concern. If a man says to his wife, "*I love you,*" but couldn't care less about what happens to her, we would rightly question his love for her. If we say that we love God, then we will hate whatever is an offense to Him. Sin seeks to destroy God's work and His Kingdom. Sin killed His Son.

So, when you say that you love God but tolerate sin, then there is every reason to question the genuineness of your love for God. You cannot love God without hating that which is set to destroy Him. True love for God manifests itself through confession and repentance. The man who loves God will be grieved over his sin and will want to confess it to God and forsake it.

Questions To Ask When Examining Your Faith

1. Do I have a settled conviction of sin?
2. Does sin appear to be an evil and bitter thing?
3. Does conviction of sin, increase within me in my walk with Christ?
4. Do I hate sin primarily because it is ruinous to my own soul or because it is an offense to God?
5. Do I grieve over sin or over its consequences?
6. Are my sins many, frequent and aggravated?
7. Do I grieve over my own sin more than the sins of others?

A person who is genuinely saved will hate sin.

3. Genuine Humility

Genuine humility is a characteristic that every born-again believer should have. Jesus said, "Blessed are those who are poor in spirit; those who mourn [for their sin], those who are meek and those who hunger and thirst for righteousness" (Matt. 5:3-6). Matthew 18:3 *says, "unless you are converted and become as little children, you will by no means enter the kingdom of heaven."* A person who

7

is full of himself is not saved; rather, a person saved denies himself, takes up his cross daily and follows Christ (Matt. 16:24).

The Lord receives those who have a broken and contrite spirit (Ps. 34:18). James wrote, *"God resists the proud but gives grace to the humble."* (James 4:6) We must come before God broken and humble, like the prodigal son. He said:

> *Father, I have sinned against heaven and in your sight, and am no longer worthy to be called your son.*

Luke 15:21

A genuine born again does not approach God with his religious achievements or spiritual accomplishments; he comes with a heart of humility.

4. Devotion To God's Glory

Children of God should be devoted to God always. Whatever we do, our aim or desire should be to see God glorified. Christians should do only those things that will bring glory to God.

5. Ceaseless Prayer

Every genuine believer in Jesus Christ will love to pray always, in obedience to the scripture that we should pray without ceasing. Jonathan Edwards once preached a sermon entitled, "Hypocrites are Deficient in the Duty of Secret Prayer." It's true. Hypocrites pray publicly because their goal is to impress people; however, they are deficient in the duty of secret prayer. True believers have a prayer life with God that is both personal and private. They regularly seek communion with God through prayer, like their Saviour, Jesus Christ.

6. Selfless Love

An important characteristic of a person saved by grace is selfless love. "If you really fulfill the royal law according to the Scripture, 'You shall love your neighbor as yourself,' you do well" (James 2:8). The Bible says:

> *Whoever has this world's goods, and sees his brother*
> *in need, and shuts up his heart from him, how can*
> *the love of God, abide in him?*

1 John 3:17

If you love God, you will hate what offends Him and love humanity. "*We passed from death to life, when we love the brethren. He who does not love his brother abides in death*" (1 John 3:14). Love is the believer's response to God's love for us; in other words, we love Him because, "*He first loved us.*" (1 John 4:19) Jesus said we will know that we are His disciples by our love for each other (John 13:35).

7. Separation From The World

True believers are not those who are ruled by worldly affections, but their affections and devotion are toward God and His Kingdom. 1 Corinthians 2:12 says:

> "*We have received, not the spirit of the world, but*
> *the Spirit who is from God, that we might know the*
> *things that have been freely given to us by God.*"

1 John 2:15 says:

> *"Love not the world, neither the things that are in the world. If any man loves the world, the love of the Father is not in him."*

True salvation separates a believer from the pursuits of worldly things. Christians are those whom God has delivered from the power of darkness and conveyed into the Kingdom of His Son (Eph. 2:1-3).

8. Spiritual Growth

True believers grow spiritually. When God begins a true work of salvation in a person, He perfects that work. *"Being confident of this very thing, that He who has begun a good work in you will complete it until the day of Jesus Christ" (Phil. 1:6).* A true Christian grows to be more like Christ. Life produces itself.

9. Obedience

Obedience is not an option for believers. Believers in Christ are to be obedient. Every branch that abides in Him shall bear good fruit (John 15:1-8). Believers in Christ are the workmanship of God, created in Christ Jesus for good works (Eph. 2:10).

Chapter 2

AMAZING GRACE FOR GENUINE SALVATION

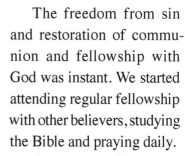

While I was courting my husband in 1994, we made a 180-degree turnaround from the path of eternal damnation to that of eternal life at a Life in the Spirit seminar. The new birth experience for us was real.

The freedom from sin and restoration of communion and fellowship with God was instant. We started attending regular fellowship with other believers, studying the Bible and praying daily.

Once we realized how close God was to us, praying to God became quite easy, like conversing with a close friend. We grew strong in the Lord and in the power of His might, and I must testify to the glory of God Almighty, that we continued to "grow in grace, and in the knowledge of our Lord and Saviour Jesus Christ."

Holy Ghost Baptism

From several Bible teachings, it became obvious that I needed to be filled with the Holy Spirit to be effective as a believer, so I started studying 1 Corinthians 12 and other scripture passages about Holy Ghost baptism.

Luke 11:9-13 says:

> *So I say to you, ask, and it will be given to you; seek, and you will find; knock, and it will be opened to you. For everyone who asks receives, and he who seeks finds, and to him who knocks, it will be opened. If a son asks for bread from any father among you, will he give him a stone? Or if he asks for a fish, will he give him a serpent instead of a fish? Or if he asks for an egg, will he offer him a scorpion? If you then, being evil, know how to give good gifts to your children, how much more will your heavenly Father give the Holy Spirit to those who ask Him?*

My Holy Ghost baptism experience made all the difference in my walk with God; living above sin became easier. I had the power to resist peer pressure and live a victorious Christian life. As I continued to seek the Lord diligently and spend time in His Word as well as worship Him in truth and in Spirit, I realized that I could effectively use my gifts of the Holy Spirit. The gifts that were dormant were also made manifest (2 Tim. 1:6).

The New King James Version says, *"Stir up the gift of God."* The gift is not something we learn; it is given to us by God and must be discovered, stirred up, and activated by us. You can stir up your gift by developing, refining, enhancing and using it.

God's Plan Of Salvation

Are you sure of where you will spend eternity? These simple facts and steps below give you 100% assurance of where you will spend eternity:

1. We Are All Sinners

For all have sinned and come short of the glory of God.

Wherefore, as by one man sin entered into the world, and death by sin; and so death passed upon all men, for that all have sinned.

Romans 3:23; Romans 5:12

2. The Penalty (Punishment) For Sin Is Death

For the wages of sin is death, but the gift of God is eternal life through Jesus Christ our Lord.

And as it is appointed unto men once to die, but after this the judgment.

Romans 6:23; Hebrews 9:27

When Adam and Eve heeded the temptation of the Serpent in the garden of Eden, sin entered the world and was passed down from generation to generation. Nevertheless, God refused to allow Satan to have the final laugh, so He made available plans even before man fell.

3. God Loves Us

> *For God so loved the world that he gave His only begotten Son, that whosoever believeth in Him should not perish, but have everlasting life.*

John 3:16

> *But God commended His love toward us, in that while we were yet sinners, Christ died for us.*

Romans 5:8

It doesn't matter what you have done, how bad you are for someone to love you, know that God loves you so much that He gave His Only Begotten Son to die for your sins, that you might have eternal life in Heaven, joy unspeakable and a life worth living.

How To Accept This Free Gift Of God

Receive His Free Gift Of Salvation

> *That if thou shalt confess with thy mouth the Lord Jesus, and shalt believe in thine heart that God hath raised him from the dead, thou shalt be saved. For with the heart man believeth unto righteousness; and with the mouth confession is made unto salvation. "For whosoever shall call upon the name of the Lord, shall be saved.*

Romans 10:9-10, 13

Salvation is a gift of God; it cannot be obtained through any other means. You cannot work or buy your way into Heaven; you must first believe in the Lordship of Christ. Salvation is a gift that everybody should receive by the grace of God through faith.

The Bible says in Ephesians 2:8-9 that,

> *For by grace are ye saved through faith; and that not of yourselves: it is a gift of God: Not of works lest any man should boast.*

Titus 3:5-7 says:

> *Not by works of righteousness which we have done, but according to His mercy He saved us, by the washing of regeneration, and renewing of the Holy Ghost; Which he hath shed on us abundantly through Jesus Christ our Saviour. That being justified by his grace, we should be made heirs according to the hope of eternal life.*

The Jailer at Philippi asked Paul and Silas when he brought them out of prison this! "...*Sirs, what must I do to be saved? And they said, believe on the Lord Jesus Christ and thou shalt be saved, and thy house.*"

To receive this gift of salvation entails bowing your head where you are, confessing your sins to God and asking for His forgiveness. You should say the prayer below:

> *Dear Lord,*
>
> *I know that I am a sinner; I believe Jesus died on the cross, shed His blood for my sins, was buried and rose from the grave. I ask You now, Lord Jesus, to come*

into my heart and take away my sins; save my soul.
Change my heart and life, Lord, to what You want me
to be. I thank You, Lord, for forgiving me of my sins
and giving me Your gift of salvation and everlasting
life by Your mercy and grace. Amen!

Claim His salvation by faith. Believe that you will be saved. Accepting Jesus as your personal Lord and Saviour is the best decision that you will ever make in your life.

Send an email to *fruitfulrehoboth@gmail.com,* so we can pray with you regularly. God Bless you.

Now That You Are Born Again

Now that you have a new life in our Lord and Saviour, these are some steps that you should take to grow in faith:

1. Regularly Read And Study Your Bible

Read and apply the precious Word of God to your life daily. The Bible says:

How sweet are thy words unto my taste!
Yea, sweeter than honey to my mouth.

Psalm 119:103

As newborn babes, desire the sincere milk of the word
that ye may grow thereby.

I Peter 2:2

The Word of God is a lamp to your feet and light to your path. It shows you the right way to take at every moment.

2. Talk To God In Prayer

Continue in prayer *and watch in the same with thanksgiving*.

Colossians 4:2

Be careful about nothing; but in everything by prayer and supplication *with thanksgiving let your requests be made known unto God*.

Philippians 4:6

Praying always with all prayer and supplication in the Spirit *and watching there unto with all perseverance and supplication for all saints*.

Ephesians 6:18

You must pray without ceasing now that you are saved!

3. Be Baptized By Immersion

Go ye therefore, and teach all nations, baptizing them in the name of the Father, and of the Son, and of the Holy Ghost.

Matthew 28:19

4. Fellowship With Other Christians In A Church Where Jesus Christ Is Preached

Not forsaking the assembling of we together, as the manner of some is; but exhorting one another: and so much the more, as ye see the day approaching.

Hebrews 10:25

5. Make The Bible Your Final Authority

> *All scripture is given by inspiration of God, and is profitable for doctrine, for reproof, for correction, for instruction in righteousness.*

2 Timothy 3:16

6. Tell Others About Christ

> *For I am not ashamed of the gospel of Christ: for it is the power of God unto salvation to everyone that believeth; to the Jew first, and to the Greek.*

Romans 1:16

Now that you have the peace that comes from the Lord Jesus Christ, tell someone about Jesus today. Don't keep the *"Greatest Gift to Mankind"* to yourself. Tell everyone you know, how Jesus has changed your life so that they too can come to know this wonderful Lord and Saviour.

The Turning Point

Notice that I took the time to discuss the steps to salvation and how you can get it. This is pivotal to regaining your original status and nature as created by God. There is an absolute need to be realigned with your Maker to be fruitful. Regardless of who you are, today is your appointed time of salvation and a turning point. The grace of God for salvation has appeared unto all men; you should gladly embrace it. Renounce the devil and all His works; dedicate your whole being to Master Jesus Christ as your Lord and personal saviour.

19

Chapter 3

Do Not Be Ignorant Of The Schemes And The Devices Of The Devil

Through my experiences in ministry, I have come to realize that a good number of Christians need a deeper knowledge and application of the word of God now than ever before. We do not apply spiritual warfare in our daily thinking, life and relationships, and lack the tools to protect ourselves from the oppression of the kingdom of darkness.

> *For we do not wrestle against flesh and blood, but against principalities, against powers, against the rulers of the darkness of this age, against spiritual hosts of wickedness in the heavenly place. Therefore take up the whole armor of God that you may be able to withstand in the evil day, and having done all, to stand.*

> **Ephesians 6:12-13**

Our thoughts either lead us towards God and good fruit or into oppression or struggle against our flesh, our unseen but real enemy.

*Be sober, be alert and cautious at all times. The
enemy of yours, the devil, prowls around like a
roaring lion seeking someone to devour.*

1 Peter 5:8

Christians are commanded to be alert. The good news is that
the death and resurrection of Jesus Christ has given us the power
to overcome the schemes of the enemy and gain freedom from the
lusts of the flesh and pride of life.

Counseling heals the soul of every wound and helps us to think
positively. Repentance helps us to resist the enemy and close the
doors to sin that Satan uses to have a foothold in our lives.

*For false Christs and false prophets will arise and
will show great signs and wonders, so as to mislead,
if possible, even the elect. "Behold, I have told you
in advance.*

Matthew 24:24

People receive information daily through various forms, such
as music, news, radio, internet and television, social media, movies,
games, books, etc. We are influenced by our environment and the
media. That is why we ought to search the full measure of the Word
from Genesis to Revelation.

*Where there is no vision, the people are unrestrained;
but happy and blessed is he who keeps the law.*

Proverbs 29:18, AMP

This is not the time for a partial truth; seek understanding, be vigilant and grow in the Word; live the word. Test all spirits; there are apostate messages everywhere, even within the church.

We are to take full measure of the Word by answering the following key questions:

What does the Bible say and mean to you? There is a need to note topics, understand the original intents from Hebrew and Greek, and consider the time and circumstances pertaining to an event that was written. Do not act like the Bible is a buffet where you choose what you only want to believe.

> *I marvel that you are turning away so soon from Him who called you in the grace of Christ, to a different gospel, which is not another; but there are some who trouble you and want to pervert the gospel of Christ. But even if we, or an angel from heaven, preach any other gospel to you than what we have preached to you, let him be accursed. As we have said before, so now I say again, if anyone preaches any other gospel to you than what you have received, let him be accursed.*

Galatians 1:6-9

You must know the Bible for yourselves and rightly divide the Word of Truth. A twist of the gospel is no gospel at all and will only lead one astray. In these last days, we are to be alert and discerning.

> *Therefore, keep watch, because you do not know the day or the hour.*

Matthew 24:13

The enemy's schemes are meant for you to doubt God and His word, thereby giving the devil access into your life. The word of God makes your sexual, moral, and behavioural beliefs come to agree with the Bible. The ugliness of sin is clearly depicted on the cross; the picture of the cross causes you to flee from sin and turn towards a loving God because you are no longer ignorant of the enemy's plots to destroy you.

Paul said that the devil takes advantage of us when we are ignorant of his devices. Many Christians are not sensitive to the spiritual world. Don't just go to church with your own plans and goals. Depend on God and His will for your life. Grow in wisdom, apply God's truth, test the spirits, discern all things and always be ready for the second coming of Christ.

Speak Positive Words

Death and life are in the power of the tongue: and they that love it shall eat the fruit thereof.

Proverbs 18:21

Words are serious business. As believers in Christ, we should be careful of the words we utter. The Bible tells us that God uses words to *"call those things that be not as though they were"* (Rom. 4:17).

We have constantly used our mouths to report the sorry state of affairs around us. Thus, the thought of calling "things that be not as though they were" seems crazy to us. It sounds crazy to declare and say that you are well when you're feeling sick, to say that you are prosperous when, in an actual sense, you are penniless.

To man, you are only lying to yourself; but to God, you have faith. A lie is designed to make someone believe something that's not true, but speaking by faith is saying words that agree with the

Word of God instead of the circumstances around you. You speak from your spirit and not from your head or mind.

Apostle Paul said in 2 Corinthians 4:13 that:

> *We have the same spirit of faith as he had who wrote,*
> *I have believed, and therefore have I spoken. We,*
> *too believe, and therefore we speak.*

The Amplified Bible

There are some folks who speak the word of God but do not back it up, and as a result, they fall flat on their spiritual faces. But just wishing and hoping won't get the job done. You've got to believe. Begin today to bring your tongue and your heart in line with the Word. Stop *"telling it like it is."* Speak and believe the promises of God. Allow the power of the word to work for you.

Do Not Be Deceived By The Schemes And Devices Of The Devil

> *In conclusion, be strong in the Lord [draw your*
> *strength from Him and be empowered through your*
> *union with Him] and in the power of His [bound-*
> *less] might. Put on the full armor of God [for His*
> *precepts are like the splendid armor of a heavi-*
> *ly-armed soldier], so that you may be able to [suc-*
> *cessfully] stand up against all the schemes and the*
> *strategies and the deceits of the devil.*

Ephesians 6:10-11, AMP

God gave you armour to protect you from the attacks of the enemy. You are armed with a belt of truth. Tie the truth of God's

Word around your waist always. Wear your helmet on your head. Guard your thinking to stay in alignment with God and walk daily with the mind of Christ.

Carry the shield of faith high to ward off every attack of the enemy. Put on the breastplate of righteousness to speak and behave like Jesus. God gave you His Word as a weapon. When you speak it out loud in affirmation and agreement with the Bible, you walk with God and retain the peace, authority, and promises of God.

Stand firm in the power of His might. Satan uses wiles to plot evil against the children of God. Wiles include scheming, craftiness, and deceit. You should be careful about your weaknesses and temperament. If you ignore the workings of the enemy and remain blind and complacent, you give Satan a place to attack and deceive you.

1 Peter 5:8-9 says:

> *Be self-controlled and alert. Your enemy the devil prowls around like a roaring lion looking for someone to devour. Resist him, standing firm in the faith...*

AMP

The Scripture above is telling Christians to be alert because their enemy is looking for the means to deceive, hinder, and torment them. Satan's plans are to stop you from receiving Jesus Christ, to deceive, oppress, hinder and torment you so you will either be led astray or be ineffective in the Kingdom of God.

Do not yield to teachings of enticement where Scriptures are interpreted out of context to prove man's point. Everything you are and do must be in agreement with the full measure of the Word.

Study to shew thyself approved unto God, a workman that needeth not to be ashamed, rightly dividing the word of truth.

2 Timothy 2:15

Jesus, The Word Of God

In the beginning was the Word, and the Word was with God, and the Word was God. He was in the beginning with God. All things were made through Him, and without Him nothing was made, that was made. In Him was life, and the life was the light of men. And the light shines in the darkness, and the darkness did not comprehend it...And the Word became flesh and dwelt among us, and we beheld His glory, the glory as of the only begotten of the Father, full of grace and truth.

John 1:1-5,14

Having a close relationship with Jesus is wrapped up in knowing Him as the Word of God. God has given you all the information and wisdom you need to discern all things in the Bible.

2 Thessalonians 2:10-11 says:

...They perish because they refused to love the truth and so be saved.

The Bible warns us that the love of many will grow cold and that apostasy will increase; the only way that you cannot be deceived is to have the mind of Christ and know God's Word that is knowing

Jesus personally. There are several ways that the enemy uses to lead you astray.

Methods The Enemy Uses To Lead You Astray

By Drawing Your Heart Away From God And His Word

Isaiah 29:13 says that the enemy will attempt to draw our hearts away from God. Satan attacks the mind to make our hearts grow cold to God. You must keep your heart open to Jesus Christ. *"… these people draw near with their mouths and honour me with their lips but have removed their hearts far from me."*

The word "heart" in Hebrew and Greek is the seat of your passion, emotions, thoughts and core beliefs. Let your time, attention, money, desires and emotions, be focused on God. Do not allow the devil to taint your view of God and His promises.

Always know that Satan is the father of lies and he wants you to turn your heart from God in unbelief.

By Doubting God

Satan makes you doubt the goodness and faithfulness of God by presenting false situations that will cause you to question God's promises.

Do not be deceived when things do not go the way that you planned. God says:

> *…My thoughts are not your thoughts, nor are your ways my ways,' says the Lord. 'For as the heavens are higher than the earth, so are my ways higher than your ways, and my thoughts than your thoughts.*

Isaiah 55:8-9

You may not always understand the situations, but resist the lies of Satan. Trust God in all situations and you shall receive every promise of God.

Through The Lust Of The Flesh, The Lust Of The Eyes, And The Pride Of Life

When your heart is drawn away from God, you begin to seek after the things of this world; your thoughts become darkened and you see things through distorted lenses.

> *Do not love the world or anything in the world. If anyone loves the world, love for the Father is not in them. For everything in the world—the lust of the esh, the lust of the eyes, and the pride of life—comes not from the Father but from the world. The world and its desires pass away, but whoever does the will of God lives forever.*

1 John 2:15-17

The enemy mainly uses the lust of the flesh, the lust of the eyes, and the pride of life to entice us to sin. Lust is a strong and intense desire.

The Lust Of The Flesh

This is anything that you recklessly pursue contrary to the will of God. It causes you to manipulate or violate your integrity. The carnal mind is an enemy to God. Our five senses are tools used by Satan to tempt us. In other words, we lust after the flesh by what we taste, touch, smell, see and hear.

Flesh, in the Bible, means anything in your heart that opposes God and His Word. There is a battle between your spirit and your flesh, daily. Man always desires for carnal things, such as immorality, the addictions that plague our nations, and for temporary satisfaction when he lives in the flesh.

> *"Then Peter said, 'Ananias, how is it that Satan has so filled your heart that you have lied to the Holy Spirit and have kept for yourself some of the money you received for the land?'"*

Acts 5:3

Be careful of your perspective about mammon. Do not put money before God. This world is your temporary home and you should seek first the Kingdom of God and its righteousness.

The Lust Of The Eyes

The lust of the eyes is a desire to possess things that appeal to your eyes. Experience often creates a faulty perception that opposes God. Your eyes can deceive you into seductive paths and pursuits, not basically sexual immorality, but by keeping your eyes focused on situations and circumstances, thereby causing distortions in your thoughts and behaviour.

The Pride Of Life

The pride of life is whatever that exalts self and causes you to be arrogant or to boast in worldly wisdom and possessions. The temptation of Jesus is a good example of pride of life.

Again, the devil took Him up on an exceedingly high mountain and showed Him all the kingdoms of the world and their glory. And he said to Him, "All these things I will give you, if you will fall down and worship me.

Matthew 4:8-9

Jesus overcame the temptations of the lust of the eyes, the lust of the flesh, and the pride of life. He focused on the Truth. He knew who He was and who God is. He also used His authority and the Word of God to overcome the schemes of the enemy.

By Diverting Your Attention From God

Do not allow the enemy to divert your heart from God. Love God always in every circumstance; love Him in good and bad times. He is with you always and will strengthen and carry you through.

Do not allow situations to ever cause you to doubt God. Remain in Him, trust His character and promises. The Bible says:

But the Lord is faithful. He will establish you and guard you against the evil one.

2 Thessalonians 3:3

Recognize how your enemy prowls around seeking to tempt you with the lust of the flesh, the lust of the eyes, and the pride of life. Seek God first, walk in His mind. Constantly renew your mind with the Word of God. Be Kingdom-minded, knowing that you have a purpose to fulfill on earth through the Holy Spirit. We cannot do anything except what He empowers, enables, and expresses the fullness of His Person through us.

Chapter 4
THE PERSON OF THE HOLY SPIRIT

M ost Christians live and die without ever enjoying the fellowship and companionship of the Holy Spirit. They'd heard about the Holy Spirit and knew some doctrines regarding the Holy Spirit, but they'd never known Him personally or experienced Him as their Helper, Comforter, and Stand by, etc.

If you are disappointed with your spiritual life, it is because you do not rely on the Holy Spirit. In this chapter, let us explore the essential role that the third person in the Trinity plays in each believer's life.

Sometimes new believers think their lives will be easier now that they are saved, but this is not usually the case. In fact, believers in Christ experience even more challenges and problems; they often wonder where God is or why He isn't answering their prayers. At such a time, a believer without the Holy Spirit might begin to feel overwhelmed and lonely.

Our Helper

Before Jesus went to the Cross, He told His disciples that He would send them a Helper. The Holy Spirit lives within every believer in Christ; and we must rely on Him in our weaknesses for strength. However, most Christians' problem is ignorance of the Holy Spirit's presence and guidance in their lives. Be willing to yield yourself to Him, and you shall freely draw from the resources of our God and Heaven. You should know that our divine Helper is always available to attend to your needs. Jesus did not leave us alone or helpless. He is always with us and actively working in our lives.

The Holy Spirit is a person (Acts 5:3-4). We know Jesus and the Father, but only a few persons know the Holy Spirit or have had a relationship with Him. The Holy Spirit is co-equal with the Father and the Son. He is not a mist, a cloud, or a strange feeling. He has feelings just like you and me. He can be grieved. He is sensitive and compassionate. He is powerful and mighty. He is the change agent on the earth—God in action in the world.

Why We Need The Holy Spirit

The Holy Spirit Gives Us Supernatural Power

Jesus, in Acts 1:8 says:

> *But you shall receive power when the Holy Spirit comes upon you. And you shall be my witnesses in Jerusalem, and in all Judea and Samaria, and to the ends of the earth.*

You should cry out now for the Holy Spirit to come upon you and fill you up.

The Holy Spirit Gives Us Supernatural Gifts

1 Corinthians 12:4-11 says:

> *There are various gifts, but the same Spirit. There are differences of administrations, but the same Lord.*

There are various operations, but it is the same God who operates all of them in all people. But the man-ifestation of the Spirit is given to everyone for the common good. To one is given by the Spirit the word of wisdom, to another the word of knowledge by the same Spirit, to another faith by the same Spirit, to another gifts of healings by the same Spirit, to another the working of miracles, to another prophecy, to another discerning of spirits, to another various kinds of tongues, and to another the interpretation of tongues. But that one and very same Spirit work all these, dividing to each one individually as He will.

When the Holy Spirit comes upon you, He gives you gifts for the edification of the Church. Inspired by the Holy Spirit, Paul tells us we should earnestly desire spiritual gifts, especially the gift of prophecy (1 Cor. 14:1).

The Holy Spirit Helps Us Build Our Faith

Jude, verse 20 says:

But you, beloved, build yourselves up in your most holy faith. Pray in the Holy Spirit.

I pray in the Spirit regularly. You edify your spirit whenever you pray in the spirit.

The Holy Spirit Gives Your Body Life And Strength

Romans 8:11 says:

> *But if the Spirit of Him who raised Jesus from the*
> *dead lives in you, He who raised Christ from the*
> *dead will also give life to your mortal bodies through*
> *His Spirit that lives in you.*

Think about that! Resurrected life is inside of you. Learn to tap into it to continue in the Kingdom race and fight the good fight of faith. The Holy Spirit is the gift of God to humanity for the purpose of being comforted.

He Teaches Us

> *But the Helper, the Holy Spirit, whom the Father will*
> *send in my name, He will teach you all things.*

John 14:26

He is a teacher who surpasses all others. He guides us as we read God's Word and helps us to interpret the word accurately. The Bible is an amazing treasure God has given us, and anytime we read it we should ask the Spirit to teach us and help us comprehend it.

He Reveals Truth To Us

> *Now we have received, not the spirit of the world, but*
> *the Spirit who is from God, so that we may know the*
> *things freely given to us by God.*

1 Corinthians 2:12

God gives us divine knowledge through the Holy Spirit from His word. Sometimes we do not understand immediately what scripture means; it is the Spirit of God who interprets to our best understanding when we continue meditating and asking God for the wisdom and understanding.

He Guides Us

> *But when He, the Spirit of truth, comes, He will guide you into all the truth.*

> **John 16:13**

The Holy Spirit is also our Guide. He helps us to discern the truth and make the right decisions. Instead of seeking other people's advice, we should first ask the Holy Spirit to direct us.

He Bears Fruit Through Us

> *The fruit of the Spirit is love, joy, peace, patience, kindness, goodness, faithfulness, gentleness, self-control.*

> **Galatians 5:22-23**

The Holy Spirit can change our attitude and habit if we will ask Him for help and genuinely desire to walk in obedience as well as bear good fruit.

He Helps Us To Remember

> *But the Helper, the Holy Spirit, whom the Father will send in My name, He will teach you all things, and bring to your remembrance all that I said to you.*

> **John 14:26**

The disciples of Jesus remembered His teachings while they were with Him with the help of the Holy Spirit. Today, we also need His help to bring to remembrance scriptures that apply to situations.

He Fills Us

"Be filled with the Spirit" (Eph. 5:18). Believers in Christ have a life that is governed and guided by the Holy Spirit. No believer has a legitimate excuse for disobeying God because the Spirit dwells in us to enable us to do the commands of God.

The Holy Spirit Helps Us To Resist Temptation

> *For if you live according to the flesh, you will die,*
> *but if through the Spirit you put to death the deeds*
> *of the body, you will live.*

Romans 8:13

Galatians 5:16 says, *"I say then, walk in the Spirit and you shall not fulfill the lust of the flesh."* If you are struggling with temptation of any kind, ask the Holy Spirit to help you overcome it. He is inside of God.

How dependent and obedient are you to the Holy Spirit? If you desire to be filled with the Holy Spirit, pray this prayer:

Father, I surrender my life to You. Fill me to overflowing with Your Spirit just as You have promised in Your word. I ask this in the name of Jesus and believe that, even now, You are pouring out Your Spirit upon me.

Chapter 5
THUS SAYS THE LORD!

I have learned that often when God speaks and it comes to pass, there is an elapsed time. What do you do while waiting for that Rhema, prophetic word, promise of God and dream to come to pass? While I was preparing for my wedding, the Lord spoke in an evening fellowship asking us to separate ourselves and consecrate our bodies to Him. He added that He would establish our marriage and use it for His glory. I wholeheartedly obeyed the word as much as I could at that time.

The Retrospect

As a young girl, I desired to know the will of God in my life especially in my marriage because any union that is in line with God's word, will stand the test of time. In his book, *Prophetic Marriages: And Other Covenants in God's Plan for the Nations*, Dr. Steve Ogan relates that *"marriage is a ministry and couples are on divine assignment.* I am concerned about how today couples are in love, and tomorrow they are divorced or separated. I realized early that marriage as ordained by God is a life commitment through thick and thin, and that in order to raise responsible children, a marriage must be stable. I had five suitors at the same time, so I prayed, and I requested prayers from different individuals and groups. The Lord answered my prayer and confirmed it; however, He told me that the journey would be bumpy.

Generally, people have this notion that if something is the will of God, it will be all rosy and thorn-free. This cuts across different aspects of life: marriage, job, ministry, mission work, and even our walk with the Lord.

Let us look closely at the case of our Lord Jesus Christ: it was the perfect will of God for Him to be born of a virgin, live on earth, do His ministry, suffer and die to redeem mankind, yet He encountered lots of resistance. At some point during His passion, He felt like the cup should pass over Him. Thank God, He quickly got over that feeling and realigned His will to the will of God the Father.

> *He who finds a wife finds what is good and receives favour from the Lord.*

Proverbs 18:22

> *God blessed them and said to them, "Be fruitful and increase in number; fill the earth and subdue it. Rule over the fish in the sea and the birds in the sky and over every living creature that moves on the ground.*

Genesis 1:28

THE WEIGHT OF THE PROMISE DETERMINES THE PERIOD OF WAITING

The Waiting Period

My husband and I expected to start having children immediately after our wedding. We looked forward to being proud parents like everyone else. However, it did not happen for us that way. Weeks

rolled into months, months rolled into a year, a year ushered in many years without any pregnancy.

Somehow, we enjoyed the promise of God in other aspects of our lives. It became clear that we needed to seek more of God's face to understand what His will was for us concerning childbearing. Amazing grace kept us going.

CATEGORIES OF THE WAITING PERIOD

Spiritual Growth

We sought the Lord more than ever; we spent a lot of time studying and meditating on the word of God, praying, worshipping and serving God and humanity. We were privileged to relate to mature Christian groups and dedicated brethren. It was truly a period of learning. We discovered among other scriptures that:

> *The thief does not come except to steal, and to kill, and to destroy. I have come that they may have life, and that they may have it more abundantly.*

John 10:10

Jesus came that we may have life and have it more abundantly. I was determined to leave no stone unturned in the area of conceiving and bearing children. God used many anointed vessels to minister deliverance to us. In Luke 4:23, Jesus said,

> *Surely you will quote this proverb to me: 'Physician, heal yourself!' And you will tell me, 'Do here in your hometown what we have heard that you did in Capernaum.*

I had to humble myself and submit to those needful ministrations. The general statement that no matter how much of an expert a surgeon is, the person cannot successfully carry out a surgery all by himself, became real in our case. The Lord used us to answer the prayers of barren women while we were waiting for our own miracle.

Deliverance

> *And the Lord shall deliver me from every evil work and will preserve me unto His heavenly kingdom: to whom be glory forever and ever Amen.*

> **2 Timothy 4:18**

People often use the term "deliverance" interchangeably with "the casting out of demons." Indeed, deliverance may entail casting out demons, but scripturally, it has a much broader meaning and deeper significance.

Biblically, Deliverance conveys an overall picture of salvation through the hand of a loving and powerful God. It describes the full impact of Jesus' birth, death and resurrection in the lives of God's people. And it signifies the fullness of freedom in Christ.

Luke 1:74-75 says:

> *To grant us that we, being delivered from the hand*
> *of our enemies, might serve Him without fear, In*
> *holiness and righteousness before Him all the days*
> *of our life.*

What Then Is Deliverance?

Deliverance means *"to deliver out of the hands of, to escape."*
This meaning illustrates God's rescue of His people from the
dominion of Satan and the world system. An example is found in
the Hebrew word *natzal,* which means "to snatch up, to take away,
to snatch out of danger, to preserve, to deliver one from danger."

Deliverance can also mean *"drawing someone to oneself."* This
concept shows that God's fervent desire is to fellowship with His
people upon whom He has set His unfathomable love. The following two verses both beautifully capture this:

> *He has delivered us from the power of darkness and*
> *conveyed us into the Kingdom of the Son of His love.*

> **Colossians 1:19 NKJV**

Deliverance is *"to deliver into the hands of... for the purpose of*
judgement." This idea involves God bringing His people into con-
frontation with their enemies so that they can defeat them in battle.
The Old Testament picture of Israel confronting the Canaanite
nation typifies the battle of the Church against the powers of darkness and the influence of the world system.

God said to the Israelites:

*And I will fix your boundary from the Red Sea to
the sea of the Philistines, and from the wilderness
to the River Euphrates; for I will deliver [give] the
inhabitants of the land into your hand, and you will
drive them out before you.*

Exodus 23:31

Deliverance also means "to have ample space between oneself
and one's enemies." It is when your enemies are beaten and brought
into subjection so that they stop oppressing and harassing you or
your land. The Bible says:

*And Thou hast not given me over into the hand of
the enemy; Thou hast set my feet in a large place.*

Psalms 31:8

The combination of the 4 definitions of deliverance above can
be summarized as:

To be removed by God from the hand of the enemy and drawn
close to Himself, to confront the enemy on God's own terms, defeat
the enemy, and gain freedom from oppression in an ample and
secure place.

Truth, The Secret Of Deliverance

Many people have gone to different places in search of freedom
from affliction and torment from the powers of darkness. Problems
often compel people to consult witch doctors, herbalists and false
prophets. Many have even joined evil societies.

Some travel within and outside different countries, spending
all the money they have just to see "great prophets and seers," yet

to no avail because they do not seek or know the truth. John 8:32 says, *"And ye shall know the truth, and the truth shall set you free."*

We overcome the battles of life by walking in the truth. Satan operates on lies and deception. To overcome him, you need the Truth. There is a saying that lies can travel thousands of years, but within a day, the truth will pursue and overtake it.

No matter how strong a satanic attack may be, as long as we tell the truth to our spouses, to ministers of God, to our brethren, neighbors and to God, we shall surely overcome. Those who exchange the truth for lies will end up multiplying their sorrows.

The barren and the poor are not always the author of these problems, rather, most of these problems emanate from the sins of their forefathers. This was the case of the children of Israel. Their forefathers sinned greatly against God. As a result, God placed a curse upon their generations.

The Bible says:

> *'Thou shall not bow down thyself to them, nor serve them, for I the Lord thy God, am a jealous God, visiting the iniquities of the fathers upon the children unto the third and fourth generations of them that hate me.'*

Exodus 20:5

> *As long as you are executing the truth to one another,"* God said, *"I shall take away all the troubles of your life.*

Zechariah 8:14-19

45

Many people who are barren today are not responsible for the cause; they cannot explain why because, before they married, they maintained a disciplined life. God is saying in Zechariah 8:14-19, that if we speak the truth among ourselves, He shall have mercy on us and heal our land.

The Bible says, *"Buy the truth and sell it not, also wisdom and instruction and understanding."* (Prov. 23:23) God says when you buy the truth; you should not sell it for anything or any reason. If you desire to receive anything from the Lord Jesus, you must buy the truth. God has given us this truth free of charge. Jesus said, "I am the way, the truth and the life, no one comes to the Father, but by Me." (John 14:6)

When you operate in the truth, Jesus dwells in you and ensures that you obtain your freedom. It is only your knowledge of the truth that shall set you free (John 8:32). The only way out of any problem is the truth and if the Son, therefore, shall make you free, ye shall be free indeed (John 8:36).

The only way to recognize a person who has Jesus Christ in his life is the truth such a person embraces. Perhaps you have not invited Jesus Christ into your heart and given Him the Lordship of your life; you can do so now, for it is the first step to obtaining freedom; be true to yourself, repent and accept Jesus Christ into your life.

Uncover all your past lies. However, you should know that when you walk in the truth, people turn against you, friends reject you, family members may reproach you, but you should press forward in the truth. It is when you are walking in truth that God works wonders in your life.

Destroying The Yoke Of Barrenness

Sometimes little things often bring mighty changes, and little steps often bring divine intervention and transformation. It is equally important to know that mountains of problems do not always need a lot of prayer and fasting; change comes into your situation when you change your ways and turn to God's way and will for your life.

In Exodus 14, the children of Israel were confronted with the greatest challenge of their time. There was the Red Sea before them, and the armies of Pharaoh were pursuing after them. All hope seemed lost. They cried out to Moses in great fear. But Moses, though confused, still had the courage to tell them:

> *Fear ye not, stand still and see the salvation of the Lord, which He will show to you today. For the Egyptians whom ye have seen today, ye shall see them again no more forever.*

Exodus 14:13

This statement sounded good enough to allay their fears, but it wasn't what the Lord required them to do. They were not to stand still but to go forward according to verse 15:

> *....And the Lord said unto Moses, wherefore criest thou unto me? Speak unto the children of Israel that they go forward.*

Exodus 14:15

Do not "*stand still,*" rather, "*go forward.*" The instruction is short and simple, and it matters so much to God.

Apostle Peter is another example of the little things that count. Every good fisherman knows that the best period to catch fish is at night, but Peter toiled all night and caught nothing. Then Jesus requested his boat in his state of depression.

Jesus made proper use of the boat, and thereafter:

> *He said unto Simon [Peter], 'Launch out into the deep, and let down your nets for a draught.' And Simon answering said unto him, 'Master, we have toiled all night and have caught nothing, nevertheless at thy word, I will let down the net.' And when they had this done, they enclosed a great multitude of fish: and their net broke.*

Luke 5:4-6

Are you seeking miracles? Do you toil all day just to make ends meet? The Lord wants you to be a blessing to others. Peter would not have gotten His miracle if he had not released his boat to the Master. Beloved, what is the Lord requesting from you?

Do you help the needy in the house of God and those around you, or do you fold your hands when there is a need to meet in the house of God? The Bible says, *"He that waters shall be watered."* (Prov. 11:25b) The little things that matter in your situation should never be overlooked. When you fail to seek a solution to your problem you gradually neglect your vision.

Song of Solomon says, *"Take out the foxes, the little foxes that spoil the vines, for our vines have tender grapes."* These foxes are so little but very destructive, God is saying that these foxes have the capacity to destroy the good things in your life. What are foxes? Foxes are wild, destructive and carnivorous animals. When a fox gets into a poultry farm, it devours all the chickens.

The Lord is warning you to steer clear of foxes so that they do not destroy the good things that he has deposited into your life. Your life is filled with potential. No wonder Genesis 1:28 says, *"And God blessed them, and God said unto them be fruitful and multiply and fill the earth and subdue it..."*

Psalm 139:14a says, *"I will praise thee for I am fearfully and wonderfully made..."* The following are some of the things that represent foxes in the lives of people:

- **Anger:** One of the most dangerous weapons of the enemy against those looking for the fruit of the womb is the spirit of anger. Anger leads to high blood pressure. Anger is a dangerous fox that God wants you to deal with. Ecclesiastes 7:9 says, *"Do not be quickly provoked in your spirit for anger resides in the lap of fools."*
- **Hypocrisy:** "For *the congregation of the hypocrites shall be desolate..."* (Job 15:34)
- **Lying**: You need to ask God to deliver you from lying. Deliver my soul, O Lord, from lying lips and from deceitful tongue. (Ps. 120:2)
- **Fear**: The acronym of fear is *False Evidence Appearing Real*. Fear opens your life for satanic attack. Satan uses the thought of receiving another negative pregnancy test result to introduce anxiety, panic, distress and terror.
- **Stubbornness**: It is being headstrong, unyielding, strong-willed and determined not to change one's attitude, behaviors or position concerning a matter. Stubbornness is a type of idolatry. *"For rebellion is as the sin of witchcraft, and stubbornness is as iniquity and idolatry. Because you have rejected the word of the Lord, He also has rejected you from being king"* (1 Sam. 15:23).
- **Unforgiveness**: It is the unwillingness to forgive the omission and commission errors of other people. It is making no allowance for the weaknesses of other people. Holding offences against someone is like drinking poison in the hope that the other person will die. *"For if you forgive men their trespasses, your heavenly Father will also forgive you.*

But if you do not forgive men their trespasses, neither will your Father forgive your trespasses" (Matt. 6:14-15).

- **Deception:** It is cheating, treachery, and deceit. It is a life of falsehood, fraud and pretense and stands in the way of true salvation. 2 Thessalonians 2:10 says, *"And with all unrighteous deception among those who perish, because they did not receive the love of the truth, that they might be saved."* You deceive yourself when you live in pretense and falsehood.

- **Fornication:** This is infidelity, unreliability and indulging in sexual intercourse outside wedlock, having sexual intimacy with a person other than your spouse. It is a sure way of allowing satanic attacks; demonic infestations, spirit spouses and sexually transmitted diseases. It is a work of the flesh and a sin against your body which is the temple of the Holy Spirit. *"Flee from sexual immorality. All other sins a person commits are outside the body, but whoever sins sexually, sins against their own body"* (1 Cor. 6:18). You will need your body to produce your fruitful vines.

- **Unfaithfulness in your Marriage**: The marriage should be undefiled.

Adultery is the act of sexual immorality or unfaithfulness among married persons. It is a killer and destroyer. It is rootless in damaging marriage relationships. It is the major cause of divorce, globally. It is a sin that God will judge. "Marriage is honorable among all, and the bed undefiled; but fornicators and adulterers God will judge" (Heb. 13:4).

- **Seek God's Face:** This is the area where many Christians fail. They would rather seek pastors than God. Some seek prophets and overseers instead of seeking God. It is not wrong to go to your pastors for counselling, but let your belief be in God and all glory should be ascribed to Him.

- **Turn From Your Wicked Ways:** There should be a process of "turning away" by forsaking your evil ways. Proverbs 28:13 says, *"He that covered his sins shall not prosper, but whoso confesses and forsaketh them shall have mercy."*

Doubt: We should believe in Jesus Christ the Son of God and have faith when we pray. Doubt can prevent us from receiving anything from God, including the fruit of the womb. "Ask and you shall receive", but when you doubt it will be hard to receive. 1 Timothy 2:8, says

I desire therefore that men pray everywhere, lifting up holy hands, without wrath and doubting." We must ask in faith. "But let him ask in faith, with no doubting, for he who doubts is like the wave of the sea driven and tossed by the wind.

How To Get Rid Of These Foxes

The only way to get rid of the little foxes that spoil the vine is the application of 2 Chronicles 7:14:

If my people which are called by my name, shall humble themselves and pray, and seek my face, and turn from their wicked ways, and then will I hear from heaven, and will forgive their sin, and will heal their land

Humility: God is no respecter of persons. No matter who or what you are, God wants you to remain humble before Him. God resists the proud and giveth grace to the humble.

Prayer: Pray fervently. Pray in the Spirit and in the name of Jesus (1 Thess. 5:17, Eph. 6:18).

Chapter 6
PERSONAL DELIVERANCE

U nderstanding self-deliverance will help you stay physically and spiritually healthy, and free from demonic pollution. You will enjoy divine health when you have the knowledge of the Word of God.

What do you do when your man of God is not around to pray for you? You are the person wearing the shoes and you know exactly the place that it hurts. Go to God in prayer. Sometimes it is not always that you should call others to pray for you.

Our environment is polluted with evil spirits and if you do not regularly cleanse your house with the blood of Jesus, demons may lodge there. If a university professor could do a ritual sacrifice to be promoted, then believers in Christ should pray and make their body as a living sacrifice unto the Lord.

The Nature Of Demons

Demons are spirits. Evil spirits leave a person through any opening in the body. This is why during deliverance prayers people may fart or emit bad odour, also called a foul spirit (Mark 9:25).

During self-deliverance prayer, it is necessary to be quiet after the prayer before ejecting those evil spirits. You just breathe in and out. Demons come out by breathing, coughing, choking, yawning, vomiting, etc. The manifestations vary according to the person and the spirit involved. All spirits that are not deeply rooted depart easily, but those deeply entrenched or stubborn will require more time, effort and the help of other believers.

Also, know that multiple spirits can be responsible for a problem. Once the spirit leaves you, there will be a change in you. Evil spirits can only stay in a person's life if they have a legal ground; therefore, keep your body pure and do not defile it. Also, constantly sanctify and cleanse your home, remove and burn down demonic altars.

1. Start with praise and worship. Sing songs of praise and worship to God! The Bible says in Psalm 100:4 that you should enter into the court of Heaven with praise. Before you plead your case and give God your strong reason why you must be delivered, praise Him.
2. Confess your sins and declare scriptures of deliverance. Some deliverance scriptures are:

Behold, I give you the authority to trample on serpents and scorpions, and over all the power of the enemy, and nothing shall by any means hurt you.

Luke 10:19

In Him we have redemption through His blood, the forgiveness of sins, according to the riches of His grace.

Ephesians 1:7

54

And the God of peace will crush Satan under your feet shortly. The grace of our Lord Jesus Christ be with you. Amen.

Romans 16:20

And they overcame him by the blood of the Lamb and by the word of their testimony, and they did not love their lives to the death.

Revelation 12:11

Having wiped out the handwriting of requirements that was against us, which was contrary to us. And He has taken it out of the way, having nailed it to the cross. Having disarmed principalities and powers, He made a public spectacle of them, triumphing over them in it.

Colossians 2:14, 15

Christ has redeemed us from the curse of the law, having become a curse for us, for it is written, and Cursed is everyone who hangs on a tree, that the blessing of Abraham might come upon the Gentiles in Christ Jesus, that we might receive the promise of the Spirit through faith.

Galatians 3:13, 14

Surely, He shall deliver you from the snare of the fowler and from the perilous pestilence.

Psalm 91:3

*...And the Lord shall deliver me from every evil work
and will preserve me unto His heavenly kingdom:
to him be glory forever and ever. Amen.*

2 Timothy 4:18

3. Break evil covenants and curses; destroy their legal hold.
You can pray like this:

   "I break any curse working against me;" or, "I break
   any covenant working against me, in the name
   of Jesus."

4. Bind all the spirits associated with ancestral covenants
and curses:

   "I bind all the spirits attached to or connected to
   the curses and covenants I have just broken, in the
   name of Jesus."

5. Lay a hand on your head and the other on your stomach or
navel and pray that the fire of the Holy Ghost should consume anything God has not planted in your body.

   Mention every organ of your body; kidney, liver,
   intestine, blood, etc. You must not rush at this level.
   Lay your hands on areas that the Spirit of God leads
   you to. Do not be afraid if you notice that you are
   swaying or staggering, etc.

6. Saturate your spirit, soul and body with the blood of Jesus
7. Demand firmly, in the name of the Lord Jesus Christ, that any spirit that is not of God should leave you. For example:

> "In the name of the Lord Jesus Christ, I come against all you hidden spirits, and I bind your activities in my life. You can no longer hide below the surface because I now recognize what you have been doing; release me, in the name of Jesus."

If you are sick you should address the spirit of infirmity directly.

> You spirit of infirmity, get out of my life now. I am redeemed by the blood of Jesus Christ, come out now. Go out by the power of the Holy Spirit. I prevail over you, in the name of Jesus.

At this point, stop talking. Open your mouth and begin to breathe in and out. Take about three to seven deep breaths to expel the spirits forcefully through your mouth and nose. This will help you to push out any deposit or impurity within your body. You may notice that you are coughing, yawning, sneezing, sweating or shedding tears, but continue.

8. After the expulsion stage, ask for a fresh in-filling of the Holy Spirit and close the session with praises. Self-deliverance keeps you from getting sick. It removes every evil seed planted in your body by the enemy; it charges your body with fire; It uproots evil plantations and builds up your confidence. Before you go to bed, you must remember these three prayer points.

- **Pray that the Walls of Fire Should Surround You**: *"For I, saith the Lord, will be unto her a wall of fire round about, and will be the glory in the midst of her"* (Zech. 2:5).
- **Pray that the Blood of Jesus Should Cover You and Your House**: *"And they overcame him by the blood of the Lamb and by the word of their testimony; and they loved not their lives unto the death"* (Rev. 12:11).
- **Pray that the Angels of God Should Encamp Around You and Your House**: *"The angel of the LORD encamped round about them that fear him and delivered them"* (Ps. 34:7).

There is no reason why self-deliverance should not be effective. However, if the person seeking deliverance is under stubborn demonic control, a family strongman or lacks enough faith or authority to defeat the oppressors because of known sin, the evil spirits will accuse the victim and defend their right.

Note that, for a person to be delivered, he or she must yearn for deliverance. Self-deliverance must not be done out of pride, shyness, fear of public embarrassment, etc. Your motives should be pure. Remember, deliverance is a process, and the time it takes depends on several things such as:

- The length of time the spirit has stayed inside a person
- The strength and reinforcement of the spirit
- The experience and degree of anointing upon those who are administering the deliverance
- The willingness of the person being delivered to be free
- Knowledge of the word of God and your level of hatred for sin

An effective self-deliverance will require a great deal of self-discipline. You may not realize the strength of your bondage until you faithfully and persistently work on it. Also, know that a foothold can become a stronghold if you fail to address it in time.

Deliverance Prayer On Breaking Covenants, Yokes And Curses

Declarations Of Relevant Scriptures

> *Having wiped out the handwriting of requirements that was against us, which was contrary to us. And He has taken it out of the way, having nailed it to the cross.*

Colossians 2:14

> *Do not be unequally yoked together with unbelievers. For what fellowship has righteousness with lawlessness? And what communion has light with darkness? And what accord has Christ with Belial? Or what part has a believer with an unbeliever? And what agreement has the temple of God with idols? For you are the temples of the living God. As God has said, I will dwell in them and walk among them. I will be their God, and they shall be my people. Therefore, come out from among them and be separate, says the Lord. Do not touch what is unclean, and I will receive you. I will be a Father to you, and you shall be my sons and daughters, says the Lord Almighty.*

2 Corinthians 6:14–18

From now on let no one trouble me, for I bear in my body the marks of the Lord Jesus.

Galatians 6:17

Therefore, if anyone is in Christ, he is a new creation; old things have passed away; behold all things have become new.

2 Corinthians 5:17

The Effective Weapon of
Deliverance is Praise.
Spend quality time in Praise
And Worship to God

Renouncing Membership Of Evil Associations

1. I withdraw and cancel my name from any evil association, with the blood of Jesus.

2. I withdraw any part of my body and blood deposited on evil altars, in the name of Jesus. I withdraw my pictures, image and soul from the altars and covens of evil associations, in the name of Jesus.
3. I reject, revoke, and renounce my membership with the Jezebel spirit, marine spirits, familiar spirits, witches and wizards, spirits of the dead and occult societies, in the name of Jesus.
4. I renounce and revoke all the oaths I took while entering evil associations, in the name of Jesus.
5. I reject and renounce all the names given to me in any of the evil associations, in the name of Jesus.
6. All the evil works I did to innocent people as a member of these evil associations, I ask the Almighty God to forgive me and wash me clean with the blood of Jesus.
7. I bind every marine spirit, Jezebel spirit and familiar spirit operating in my life with chains and fetters of God, and cast you out into the unquenchable fire of God, in the name of Jesus.
8. I break any covenant binding me with any evil association, in the name of Jesus.
9. I break all inherited covenants and covenants that I consciously and unconsciously entered into in the name of Jesus.
10. I break and cancel every evil mark, incision and writing placed on my body as a sign of my membership or initiation with the blood of Jesus I purify my body, soul and spirit with Holy Ghost fire, in the name of Jesus.
11. I break all covenants inherited from my paternal and maternal forebears, in the name of Jesus.
12. Lord, break down every evil foundation of my life and rebuild a new one on Christ, the Rock.
13. I purge myself of all evil foods I have eaten, with the blood of Jesus.

14. I resign my position in any of these associations and with-draw my services and responsibilities permanently, in the name of Jesus.
15. I return any property of evil associations at my disposal in the name of Jesus.
16. I hereby confess my separation from evil associations, in the name of Jesus.
17. Holy Spirit, build a wall of fire round about me that will make it completely impossible for these evil spirits to come to me again.
18. I command the fire of God to roast and burn to ashes every evil bird, snake, or any other animal attached to my life by evil association, in the name of Jesus.
19. I dismantle every hindrance, obstacle or blockage put in by the devil, in the name of Jesus.
20. All the doors of blessings and breakthrough that have been shut against me due to my involvement with evil associations, I command you to open, in the name of Jesus.

Deliverance From Curses

1. I break and cancel every inherited curse, in the name of Jesus
2. I break and cancel every curse placed upon me by my parents, in the name of Jesus.
3. I break and cancel every curse, spell, hex, enchantment, bewitchment, incantation placed upon me by any evil association, in the name of Jesus.
4. I break and revoke every blood and soul-tie covenant and yokes attached to me and my family in the name of Jesus.
5. Lord, remove from me all the curses placed upon my family as a result of evil associations and involvement, in the name of Jesus.

6. I purge myself of all the evil foods I have eaten in the evil world with the blood of Jesus and purify myself with the fire of the Holy Ghost, in the name of Jesus.
7. I declare my body, soul and spirit "out of bounds" for all evil spirits, in the name of Jesus.

Deliverance From Spirit Husband Or Wife

1. I divorce and renounce my marriage with evil spirits, in the name of Jesus.
2. I break all covenants entered into with any spirit spouse, in the name of Jesus.
3. I break every blood and soul-tie covenant with any spirit spouse, in the name of Jesus.
4. I command the thunder of God to burn to ashes the spiritual wedding gown, ring, photographs and marriage certificates, in the name of Jesus.
5. Let the thunder of God burn to ashes the children born to the marriage, in the name of Jesus.
6. I withdraw my blood, sperm or any other part of my body deposited in the altar of the spirit spouse, in the name of Jesus. I bind every spirit spouse tormenting my life and earthly marriage with the chains and fetters of God and cast you into the pit, never to come into my life again, in the name of Jesus.
7. I return all your property in my possession including the dowry and whatsoever was used for the marriage and covenants, in the name of Jesus.
8. I use the blood of Jesus to drain myself of all evil deposits in my body during any spiriual sexual intercourse.
9. Lord, send the Holy Ghost fire into my root to burn down all unclean things deposited in it by the spirit spouse in the name of Jesus.

10. I break the head of the snake deposited by the spirit husband or wife to harm me in the name of Jesus.

11. I purge out with the Blood of Jesus every evil material deposited into my womb to prevent me from having children on earth, in the name of Jesus.

12. Lord, repair and restore every bit of damage done to any part of my body and my earthly marriage by the spirit husband or wife, in the name of Jesus.

13. I reject and cancel every curse, evil pronouncement, spell, jinx, enchantment and incantation placed upon me by the spirit husband or wife, in the name of Jesus.

14. I take back all my earthly belongings in the custody of the spirit husband or wife, in the name of Jesus.

15. I command the spirit husband or wife to permanently turn his or her back on me forever, in the name of Jesus.

16. I renounce and reject the name given to me by the spirit husband or wife, in the name of Jesus.

17. I hereby declare and confess that the Lord Jesus Christ is my Husband till eternity, in the name of Jesus.

18. I soak myself in the blood of Jesus and cancel the evil mark or writings placed on me, in the name of Jesus.

19. I am free from the stronghold and domineering power and bondage of the spirit spouse, in the name of Jesus.

20. I paralyse the spiritual evil remote control power being used to destabilise my earthly marriage and to hinder me from bearing children in the name of Jesus.

Breaking Covenants And Yokes

1. I break every covenant with water spirits and the yokes attached to them, in the name of Jesus.

2. I break and cancel every covenant with any idol and the yokes attached to them, in the name of Jesus.

3. I break and cancel any evil covenants entered into by my parents on my behalf and all the yokes attached to them, in the name of Jesus.

4. I command the fire of God to roast the forces of hindrance and obstacles and paralyse their power, in the name of Jesus.

5. I confess that my deliverance shall remain permanent in the name of Jesus.

Chapter 7
PHASES OF THE JOURNEY TO VICTORY

Prayer

By divine connection, I established a spiritual relationship with a particular friend. We prayed without ceasing, upheld each other in everything that pertains to life and godliness through prayer.

My friend's major challenge was to understand the purpose of God for her life and for the salvation of her husband. God honoured His Word in our lives and answered every single prayer we brought to Him.

Today, my friend and her husband run a blossoming deliverance ministry where God is reaching numerous people and families.

Hearing From God

As I consistently sought the Lord for who He is, I grew in my intimacy with Him. I moved from merely seeking a miracle to enjoying spending time in His presence. I realized that I had a personal relationship with Him. It was amazing how the Lord began to speak to me concerning the fruit of the womb when it was no longer my main focus—that is, I wasn't anxious and distracted because of that. I knew without a shadow of a doubt that in His time He makes all things beautiful. The Lord spoke to me through dreams, revelations, Rhema, and prophecy. When I became intimate with Him, the Lord said this to me:

- *He was preparing us to bring forth godly seeds.*
- *We needed to wait for His appointed time.*
- *Our children would be released when we got to our mission field.*
- *We did not need any form of medical intervention; that He would do it and take all the glory.*
- *Through our experience, we would be anointed to bless others in the area of childbearing.*

Discovering Your Mission And Purpose

I read a book that was a guide to a forty-day spiritual journey that enabled me to discover the answer to life's most important question: Why am I on earth? By the end of that journey, I knew

God's purpose for my life and I understood how all the pieces of my life can fit together. Having this perspective reduced my stress, simplified my decisions, increased my satisfaction, and most importantly, prepared me for eternity. I encourage you to intentionally set some time aside daily with a goal to deepen your relationship with God through worship, Bible study and daily quiet time.

Mine was for forty days; the Bible is clear that God considers forty

days a spiritually significant time. Whenever God wants to prepare someone for his purposes, He first takes him out for forty days:

- Noah's life was transformed by forty days of rain.
- Moses was transformed by forty days on Mount Sinai.
- The spies were transformed by forty days in the Promised Land.
- David was transformed by Goliath's forty-day challenge.
- Elijah was transformed when God gave him forty days of strength from a single meal.
- The entire city of Nineveh was transformed when God gave the people forty days to change.
- Jesus was empowered after spending forty days in the wilderness.
- The disciples were transformed after spending forty days with Jesus before His ascension.

It was during this waiting period that I discovered my mission; I received a divine answer to, *"Why am I on earth?"* My entire life was transformed into a purpose-driven life. I became completely sold out to the Lord and His Kingdom agenda. The revelations, dreams, visions and rhema from the Lord while we waited on Him were quite enormous and reassuring. His words were really our spiritual anchor that kept us hopeful, joyfully loving and serving Him. Specifically; the Lord said, *"... you are an ambassador in a French-speaking country..."* So, as we were preparing to go to Canada, God revealed that we would have our children there.

Period Of Hard Training

God described the victory journey some months before I conceived my first miracle baby as periods of a trial of our faith. Hebrews 11:1 and 11:6 say:

Now faith is the substance of things hoped for, the evidence of things not seen.

... but without faith, it is impossible to please Him, for he that cometh to God must believe that He is and that He is a rewarder of them that diligently seek Him.

By faith, I believed without a shadow of a doubt that our chil-dren were already released. At one point, the Holy Spirit said I need to stop asking God to bless me with the fruit of the womb, rather that I should begin to pray into the destinies of the children, specifically speaking into existence what I desire for each of them.

So, we began to fervently speak into the destinies of our children, declaring the Word of God and asking Him to establish His Word in their lives. We would often pray with Psalm 127:35, that says:

Children are a heritage from the LORD, offspring a reward from him. Like arrows in the hands of a warrior are children born in one's youth. Blessed is the man whose quiver is full of them. They will not be put to shame when they contend with their opponents in court.

Other Scriptures We Prayed With

Your wife will be like a fruitful vine within your house; your children will be like olive shoots around your table.

Psalms 128:3

He will love you and bless you and increase your numbers. He will bless the fruit of your womb, the crops of your land—your grain, new wine and olive oil—the calves of your herds and the lambs of your flocks in the land he swore to your ancestors to give you. You will be blessed more than any other people; none of your men or women will be childless, nor will any of your livestock be without young.

Deuteronomy 7:13-14

And none will miscarry or be barren in your land, I will give you a full life span.

Exodus 23:26

Confession Is Possession

There are over 3000 Scriptures concerning words, mouth, tongue and lips that reemphasize what God wants us to know and do. Confession in this context is agreeing with God; saying and believing what God has already said.

We must pray in agreement with God's Word. We have God's Word for every area of our lives; our words should agree with God's written Word. The Bible is the will of God; we must give voice to it in our prayers and our everyday lives. It is absolutely necessary to be in agreement with the Word of God.

Phase Of Taunting

People will always be humans and will speak out of the abundance of their "faithless" heart. 1 Samuel 1:6-7 says:

> *Because the LORD had closed Hannah's womb, her rival kept provoking her in order to irritate her. This went on year after year. Whenever Hannah went up to the house of the LORD, her rival provoked her till she wept and would not eat.*

Peninnah made herself Hanna's adversary just because she was yet to have children. I experienced exactly the same treatment and endured taunted statements and questions such as; *"Are you still like this?" "You are a man." "Don't you want children?" "Do you ask God to give you children?" "How come you always pray for everyone else rather than yourselves?" "Intercessors for Nigeria, have you prayed for yourselves?" "What are you doing to solve your problem?" "Is it your sins that have made you remain childless?" "God is punishing you." "You cannot stay in this marriage; though you are legally married, you can still be sent away."*

Response

You need to bring back every taunting and sarcastic comment to God in prayer; present it to the Father as you spend quality time with Him. Only God can destroy their intended negative effects and reassure you by His spirit, to believe His report.

Loneliness

I was isolated by brethren, friends, colleagues, neighbours and those who were privileged to have their children right after they got married. For instance, people kept back their children from me, neighbour's children would feel free to spend time with me only when their parents were not home. The moment their parents returned, they would speedily leave before they could be seen.

Though I felt pained being treated that way, I endeavoured to take care of the children whenever such occasion arose. I would feed them, play with them, and generally guide them without expecting any form of acknowledgment. Some women who were waiting, like me, once they conceived, would hide it and disconnect from me. Some extended family members who had children consciously kept them away from us.

Response To Isolation

We must realize that the Lord Jesus Christ is a friend at all times indeed. God's answer to loneliness is a quality relationship with Him. Let your prayers become more conversational and less formal in His presence. Loneliness is God's way of drawing us closer to Him and forcing us to reach out to other people.

The period of waiting for the fulfillment of God's Word can be lonely. Ensure you overcome the distractions that come with walking in faith and believing God against all odds. Develop the habit of walking and talking with the Lord through your normal daily activities. Look unto Jesus Christ, the Author and Finisher of your faith. And you shall not be moved by any negative things you see, hear or experience. Cultivate the presence of the Holy Spirit; learn to rely on Him every step of the way.

Rejection

I must acknowledge one or two brethren who brought their children over for vacations, holidays and weekends; it was really a great privilege. My husband loves children so much that anytime he sees a child you can see the excitement and satisfaction he derives from interacting with children.

Response

As a teacher in one of the high-end private schools in the nation, God provided the opportunity for me to pour out my life, raising children from kindergarten to Grade 4 over a period of ten years. Teaching is my passion, not just a profession; there was such a connection between the students and me that I was constantly asked if

some of them were my biological children. I was in charge of the pre-school department for about four years; with over 80 children under my care. As soon as they saw me, they would rush to be the first to hug, kiss and express their love to me; it was amazing how God re-channelled my energy/focus within the years I taught those pupils.

Most of the parents did not even know that I was yet to have my own children; I had this overflowing joy, peace, fulfillment and satisfaction at my job. You may not be a teacher, but I highly recommend volunteering some of your time in the service of children.

Colossians 3:23-24 says:

Whatever you do, work at it with all your heart, as working for the Lord, not for men, since you know that you will receive an inheritance from the Lord as a reward. It is the Lord Christ you are serving.

Practical Obedience By Faith

As Christians, we have two options in life; either to walk by faith or by sight. Walking by sight means we must have all the facts and see how God's plan for our lives will unfold before we step out in obedience. If the outcome is secure, we will proceed.

On the other hand, walking by faith requires that we trust the Lord and His will for us, even if it is risky, unknown, or difficult. God wants us to depend on Him, trusting Him to direct our steps one at a time, so we can reach the destination He has planned for us.

At one point, in obedience to the promise of God and to demonstrate my unalloyed faith in God Almighty, I began to purchase newborn items, like clothes. Besides that, I bought a very beautiful solid wood baby crib and set it up in my baby's room in anticipation. Intermittently, I would pray and speak the Word of God over everything in that room, calling into being that which does not yet exist.

One way we can measure our spiritual growth is by how readily we trust the Lord and follow through with obedience. Obedience is a major theme in the Bible because it is so important that we learn to do what God says.

Most of what we are experiencing in life right now is the result of either our obedience or our disobedience. If we have trusted the Lord and followed Him faithfully, we are becoming the person He wants us to be and fulfilling His will for our lives.

Discovering True Liberty Through Surrender

Maybe you are wondering when your journey of barrenness will end. Perhaps it is taking too long and you are wondering

when this cycle of waiting will end.

Though it may seem long, hard and often painful, God shall do something divinely phenomenal in you during this season. God transformed my desires and revealed His everlasting, all-surpassing love. Through the experience of waiting on the Lord for children, God took me on a journey where I surrendered completely to Him and trusted Him, whether or not I had a baby.

I learned how to worship Him while my hands were empty, and my womb was "barren." Months of disappointment went by, but I relied on God's will and His promises. I actively pursued God's plan for my life and began to live the scripture in 1 Thessalonians 5:16-18 which says:

> *Rejoice always, pray without ceasing, and give*
> *thanks in all circumstances; for this is the will of*
> *God in Christ Jesus for you.*

I realized that God was calling me to embrace and rejoice in who He is, trust in His goodness, despite my infertility, and to be thankful. Intentionally, I had to always find reasons to thank God in my life.

Gratitude Changed My Perspective

I thanked God in every situation. I began speaking into the life of my children rather than asking. I thanked Him in advance

for my children and I thanked Him for making me be the mother of special children with divine purpose. I also thanked God for His unique plan for me and for the great people placed in my life that He had already entrusted to me.

This life of gratitude completely transformed my perspective and opened my eyes to see what God was already doing in my life. It opened my heart to trust Him and to desire His will above mine (Prov. 3:5-6). I embraced all of Him, even though I was yet to get pregnant; I worshipped, but with open hands because only a hand that is open can receive from the Lord.

The longing I felt within me for a child could only ever be satisfied in Him. I found peace and joy in Him alone and not in what I wanted. "Infertility" was no longer like a death sentence, as I knew assuredly that only God could give me children in His time, and that even though my womb was empty, my heart was full of life and God—I was alive in Him and He in me.

Hope For Your Journey

Some of you might be wondering, *"How could I be happy or thankful about this and find joy in this?"* I understand that. It took me *years* to loosen the grip I had on my life and childbearing. It was really hard, but the grace of God enabled me to get to that level of thanksgiving.

Truths To Hold On To In Times Of Trial

Know That God Is Sovereign Over All

Human beings will always tell you that you are in control of your life. Nevertheless, God's Word tells us otherwise. We are only stewards. Therefore, there are some things that are not within our power; we must first consult with our Director before fixing it. Rest in the fact that God is in charge of your life. Only He can fix your life appropriately. The Bible says that,

> *Your eyes saw my unformed body; all the days ordained for me were written in your book before one of them came to be.*

Psalm 139:16

God Is Doing What's Best For You, Even When You Can't See It

We often think we know what is best for us, but the truth is that only God does. We can rest in the fact that God is full of wisdom and love toward us, and He sees things that we cannot. Romans 8:28 says:

> *And we know that for those who love God all things work together for good, for those who are called according to his purpose.*

God's Timing And Ways Are Infinitely Better Than Ours

Again, we have to believe that God's timing is perfect. There are things we can never understand until we meet God face to face. Prophet Isaiah got this understanding and declared:

> *For as the heavens are higher than the earth, so are my ways higher than your ways and my thoughts than your thoughts.*

Isaiah 55:9

God knows when your body can handle a pregnancy. Be rest assured that He is working on you to make all things beautiful in His time. Therefore, while trusting and waiting on Him, keep thanking Him for seeing ahead.

Know That Trials Transform Our Character And Makes Us To Hope In God

No one likes tough times; but actually, tough times or trials produce good in our lives. God uses the thorns of life as his primary means to speak to us, to reveal our idols and ultimately to shape us to be more like Him. Apostle Paul speaking to the Romans said:

> *We rejoice in our sufferings, knowing that suffering produces endurance, and endurance produces character and character produces hope.*

Romans 5:3-4

Again, the Bible tells us to rejoice when we suffer. How is that possible? In our times of suffering, we draw our joy from God and not from our circumstances. Suffering has a way of setting us free from the illusion that our dreams and desires are meant to be fulfilled on this earth. We realize through suffering that we were made for His Kingdom and our purpose is fulfilled as we hope in God and not in ourselves.

> *Count it all joy, my brothers when you meet trials of various kinds, for you know that the testing of your faith produces steadfastness. And let steadfastness have its full effect, that you may be perfect and complete, lacking in nothing.*

James 1:2-4

My prayer for you is that as you walk this road, you should surrender completely to God. That may be scary. However, to surrender is not for you to *give up*, but it means to *give* it *over* to God. Jesus modelled surrender in His prayer:

Let not my will, but yours be done. For I am Yours.

Luke 22:42

There is such freedom and joy when we let God take that giant

burden off our shoulders and the yoke off our neck. This is the beauty of surrender. To surrender is not letting your dreams fall by the wayside. But it is to let God hold your dreams and count every hair on your head (Matt. 10:30). God cares about your desire to be a mom or dad. He will accomplish His purpose for you in His time. He is indeed worthy of our worship.

Chapter 8
DESPERATE WOMEN IN THE BIBLE WHO STRUGGLED TO CONCEIVE A CHILD

I n scripture, women specifically healed of barrenness had several things in common: they were desperate, they cried out to the Lord, and they brought forth either a prophet or a deliverer of the nation. The women are: Sarah, Rebekah, Hannah, Elizabeth, Rachel, Monoah's wife and Ruth.

Sarah–Mother Of Isaac

Sarah struggled to conceive a child for over seventy years, even though God had promised her a child. When Sarah was ninety years old, God reassured her of His promise and the Bible says that Sarah laughed for she was much too old. But God replied:

> *Why did Sarah laugh and say, 'Will I really have a child, now that I am old?' Is anything too hard for the Lord? I will return to you at the appointed time next year, and Sarah will have a son.*

> **Genesis 18:13-14**

God is not hindered by our physical limitations, what is impossible with men is possible with God. Sarah came to truly believe God's Promise when she gave birth to a son, Isaac. The Bible says that Sarah had faith in God:

> *And by faith even Sarah, who was past childbearing age, was enabled to bear children because she considered him faithful who had made the promise. And so, from this one man, and he as good as dead, came descendants as numerous as the stars in the sky and as countless as the sand on the seashore.*

> **Hebrews 11:11-12**

Your acts of trust and faith have a lasting effect. Sarah became the mother of many nations and an everlasting royalty, from where King David and Jesus Christ came.

Declaration Prayers

> *God of Sarah, indeed there is nothing too hard for you, I receive faith to conceive and bear a healthy child in Jesus' name.*

> *Oh God, help my unbelief that I may obtain your promise of supernatural childbirth in Jesus' name.*

Four Lessons To Learn From Sarah

1. Infertility Is Not the Result of Past Sin.

Sarah laughed at God when she heard the prophecy of her son's birth (Gen. 18:12-15), yet God kept to His Promise and saved her. God doesn't treat us according to our sins; His grace and mercy give us gifts that we do not deserve. Isaac actually means "laughter," perhaps a nod to his parents' disbelief transformed into joy.

2. Don't Let The Desire To Have Children Destroy Your Relationship With Your Spouse.

Sarah's desperation to have a family made her give her servant Hagar to Abraham, so she could have a son through her. Hagar and Abraham's relationship eventually caused a wedge between Sarah and her husband (Gen. 16:1-6). Is there anything you are doing out of desperation? Getting pregnant is not worth sacrificing the peace of your home and intimacy with your spouse. Sex in marriage is not just about making babies; it's about becoming one with the other person.

3. God's Timing Is Always Right.

If Sarah had not given birth to Isaac when she did, he wouldn't have met Rebekah, his wife. Sarah didn't know it then, but the timing of Isaac's birth created the family tree of Jesus. Your family will grow at the right time because our God is the God of perfect timing (Rom. 5:6).

4. God Will Ultimately Fulfill His Promises.

God's Word says clearly in Isaiah that His thoughts are higher than ours; His ways different than ours; and He will always, without fail, accomplish what He has promised (Isa. 55:8-11). Even Jesus told His brothers that His timing was different from theirs. (John 7:6-8) Do not fear. God cannot lie. He will break protocol just to ensure that His Word is established.

Rebekah–The Mother Of Esau And Jacob

Isaac and his wife, Rebekah, were happily married, but Rebekah was barren. Isaac married Rebekah when he was forty and they had their twin sons twenty years later. Isaac prayed to God for his wife, and God heard the prayer and Rebekah became pregnant.

Isaac prayed to the Lord on behalf of his wife, because she was childless. The Lord answered his prayer, and his wife Rebekah became pregnant. The babies jostled each other within her, and she said, "Why is this happening to me?" So, she went to inquire of the Lord. The Lord said to her, "Two nations are in your womb, and two peoples from within you will be separated; one people will be stronger than the other, and the older will serve the younger.

Genesis 25:21-24

Rebekah, Isaac's wife just like Sarah, Isaac's mom, had a delay in childbirth.

Like Hannah, when your spirit is utterly broken and contrite, desperately fast and pray, also, to catch a vision beyond your personal desire for a child. Hannah touched the heart of God when she met God's need for a prophet in the land. Brokenness and desperation made her give Samuel back to God. Brokenness is a state of absolute surrender to God's will; it propels us to die to self in obedience to the Holy Spirit's direction.

Prayers And Declarations

O God bring me to a place of brokenness where I will submit my will to have a child completely unto You, in Jesus' name.

Holy Spirit of the Highest God, open my eyes to see the need of God while seeking solutions to my problems, in Jesus' name.

O Lord, please grant me the grace to fulfill my promise and vow to You, in Jesus' name.

Fruitful Vine and Olive Shoots

Hannah–Mother Of Samuel

Hannah longed to have a son for many years, but she never gave up hope. She prayed very often and had faith in the Lord. She vowed to God that if He opened and healed her womb and gave her a son, that the child would forever serve the Lord. She prayed thus:

> *Lord Almighty, if you will only look on your servant's (herself) misery and remember me, and not forget your servant but give her a son, then I will give him to the Lord for all the days of his life.*

1 Samuel 1:11

God answered her prayer and gave her Samuel. Even though it must have been incredibly painful for her, she fulfilled her promise to God. She took Samuel to be raised by Eli, the priests at Shiloh.

She visited him every year, and always took a linen garment, called an Ephod, which is a symbol of priestly status.

Ask God to use you to meet a need, as in the case of Hannah; there was a need for a prophet of God and Hannah desperately needed a son. The moment she prayed according to the will of God and made a vow to consecrate her son unto His service, her miracle was released. Often, God uses a delay to break our hearts and to work out His perfect timing in the circumstances around us. At other times, we have delay because we ask with the wrong motives.

> *"You ask [God for something] and do not receive it, because you ask with wrong motives [out of selfishness or with an unrighteous agenda], so that [when you get what you want] you may spend it on your [pleasure-seeking] desires."*

James 4:3 AMP

Elizabeth- The Mother Of John The Baptist

Elizabeth was the mother of John the Baptist. Her story is recorded in Luke 1:7-13, 57. Similar to Sarah, Elizabeth gave birth to John the Baptist in her old age. She must have given up on the hope of becoming a mother. Being barren would have been a reproach and a source of grief to Elizabeth, but God changed all that.

> *Elizabeth expressed her appreciation for God's blessing: "Thus the Lord has dealt with me, in the days when He looked on me, to take away my reproach among people."*

Luke 1:25

- **Rachel, the mother of Joseph and Benjamin–**Genesis 29:31, 30:1, 22-24, 35:16-18.
- **Manoah's wife–**She is the mother of Samson. Her story is seen in Judges 13:2-24.
- **Ruth–She** is the mother of Obed, the daughter-in-law of Naomi. See her story in Ruth 4.

Travailing In Prayer

"Travail" is an intense intercession given by the Holy Spirit whereby an individual or group is gripped by the things of God. The individual or group labours with Him for an opening to bring forth a new life. Webster's New World Dictionary defines travail as: *"very hard work, the pains of childbirth, intense pain, agony, to toil, to suffer the pains of childbirth."*

This definition describes both physical and spiritual travail. You travail after you have carried a burden in your heart for a period of time and suddenly your eyes are filled with tears while praying for the promise of God to come to pass in your life. You are greatly relieved when the burden is lifted off your heart and shoulders.

The prayer of travail is an "opening" to bring forth a measure of life or growth. Just as the "opening" of the natural womb is enlarged to bring forth the baby, so travailing in prayer creates an "opening" or "way," to bring forth answers to your request. A way opens for life, newness, change, or growth whenever a child of God travails in prayer.

Accounts Of Agonizing And Wrestling In Prayer

Only a few persons have an understanding of wrestling in prayer. It is only when you have revelations that you can recognize what is at stake in the kingdom of God and you make the effort to combat it in warfare prayer.

In warfare, you push through a host of difficulties and reach beyond the natural realm to the very throne of God with all your strength. You lay hold of God's grace and power as a passion of your soul. Jacob wrestled with the angel until he got the blessing, even though the angel broke his thigh.

> *Jacob was left alone, and a man wrestled with him until daybreak. And when he saw that he had not prevailed against him, he touched the socket of his thigh; so, the socket of Jacob's thigh was dislocated while he wrestled with him. Then he said, 'Let me go, for the dawn is breaking.' But he said, 'I will not let you go unless you bless me'.*

Genesis 32:24-26

Your tenacious and persevering prayer will eventually pay off.

Surviving Infertility On Mother's Day

Mother's Day is a day set aside to celebrate and honour mothers, motherhood, maternal bonds, and the influence of mothers in society. It is celebrated on various days in many parts of the world, most commonly in the months of March or May.

We may not realize it, but Mother's Day can be hard for people who are struggling with infertility, miscarriages and the loss of a mother. There is a need to think about the broken and barren women on Mother's Day.

While Mother's Day is a celebration for some women, it is a day of sorrow and pain for others going through struggles and challenges; it is a day laden with emotional loneliness, psychological trauma and anguish for women who are plagued with infertility.

Mother's Day should be an opportunity to reach out to the women who are yet to have children; those who have lost  their moms and those who are emotionally down because of miscarriage.

Ways To Support Your Friend Who Is Dealing With Infertility

Did you know that June is World Infertility Awareness Month? I didn't know this until recently. I love the concept because infertility is a worldwide issue. Here are some suggestions on how to support your infertile friends:

Just Listen

Do not give any advice because they have heard it all. They know how babies are made, and trust me, they've tried that. Just listen to how your friend is feeling, because it's so lonely to go through this alone.

Give A Hug

A nice hug can go a long way. It shows how much you care about a person's feelings without saying a word—a universal sign of friendship.

Admit That You Don't Understand

People say they understand when they really don't. Your friend would much rather want to hear that you don't understand.

Offer To Go With Her To Appointments

You have no idea how awful your friend feels visiting the doctors. Accompanying him or her to the hospital would be a very kind gesture as the waiting room at most fertility clinics is dead silent.

Find Out Her Mental, Physical And Emotional States

Infertility can be physically, emotionally, mentally, and financially crippling, especially on Mother's Day, Father's Day, Thanksgiving, etc.

Don't Try to Solve the Problem

Just because something worked for you or for someone else, does not mean it will work for everyone struggling with infertility. There are several types of infertility with different treatments.

Chapter 9
THE FRUITFUL VINE

There are many stories, promises, accounts, prophecies and parables about fruit in the Bible. Fruit is mentioned in over forty of the sixty-six Books of the Bible.

It is mentioned in the first chapter of Genesis and the last chapter in Revelation. Indeed, God is a Master Gardener; more than that, He is the Creator of fruit.

Fruit is a product of a seed sown. The fruit of a plant or tree is its edible produce. The fruit of an animal or person is the offspring. In a figurative sense, fruit is the product of our efforts and labours. In other words, it is the result of our actions.

Be Fruitful

The first blessing of God to Adam and Eve was, "Be fruitful" (Gen. 1:29). God wants mankind to bear fruit and multiply in all areas of life; not just in the area of procreation.

In the account of creation, we are told that God made every plant, tree and animal to reproduce after their kind. Even Adam *"became the father of a son in his own likeness, according to his image,"* just as God created Adam *"in his own image"* (Gen. 1:27). Man is designed by God to create—that is, to bear fruit.

Bible Passages That Describe Man As Trees, Plants And Vine

God referred to men as tree, plant and vine in the following Bible Passages:

> *How blessed is the man who does not walk in the counsel of the wicked, nor stand in the path of sinners, nor sit in the seat of scoffers! But his delight is in the law of the Lord, and in His law, he meditates day and night. He will be like a tree firmly planted by streams of water, which yields its fruit in its season and its leaf does not wither.*

> **Psalm 1:1-3**

> *The righteous man will flourish like the palm tree; he will grow like a cedar in Lebanon. Planted in the house of the Lord, they will flourish in the courts of our God. They will still yield fruit in old age; they shall be full of sap and very green.*

> **Psalm 92:12-14**

> *The Lord called your name, 'A green olive tree, beautiful in fruit and form'.*

> **Jeremiah 11:16**

Blessed is the man who trusts in the Lord, whose confidence is in him. He will be like a tree planted by the water that sends out its roots by the stream. It does not fear when heat comes; its leaves are always green. It has no worries in a year of drought and never fails to bear fruit.

Jeremiah 17:7-8

The moment we receive the *"seed"* of God's Word in our hearts, God expects fruit from us. As a Gardener, God expects the trees that are planted in His Garden to bear good fruit (Luke 8:11).

Abiding In The Vine

Psalm 128:2-3 says that one of the blessings upon the man who fears God is that his wife will be *"like a fruitful vine."* Proverbs 31 examines ways in which a wife can be a "fruitful vine." The fruit of the womb is also a blessing of the Lord (Ps. 127:3). The church, the bride of Christ, has the incredible honour of bearing fruit for God (Rom. 7:14).

You and I are not just designed to bear fruit *for* God, as if it were something we had to do by our own power, we are designed to bear the fruit *of* God, as a direct result of being intimate with him. In natural marriage, it is through physical intimacy with her husband that a woman bears the *"fruit of the womb."* In the same way, it is only through an intimate relationship with the Spirit of Jesus Christ that we can truly bear the fruit of God.

It was this process of being intimate with The Spirit of God that Jesus referred to in John 15:4 when He said:

*Abide in Me, and I in you. As the branch cannot
bear fruit of itself unless it abides in the vine, so
neither can you unless you abide in me.*

1 John 3:23-24 tells us that we "abide" in Jesus by believing in
Him and keeping His commandments, and that as a result of our
abiding in Him, He, in turn, abides in us through the presence of
His Spirit within us.

The Fruit Of God In Us

We have established that God expects us to bear fruit and that
He intends for us to "inspect" the fruit of others. But what exactly
is the "fruit" that we are to bear as the bride of Christ—his *"fruitful
vine"*—and how can we recognize this fruit in our own lives and
in the lives of others?

In essence, it is everything that is accomplished by the presence
of God's Word and Spirit within us. From the moment God's Word
takes root in our hearts and His Holy Spirit comes to dwell in our
lives, He begins to bear fruit in us.

There are several passages that refer to this fruit of God's presence in our lives. In Isaiah 61:3, God refers to his people as, *"Trees
of righteousness, the planting of the Lord."* Just as an apple tree
produces apples and a cherry tree produces cherries, a "tree of righteousness" is one that produces righteousness. The fruit of righteousness will be evident in the life of anyone who is born of God's
Spirit, for it is only *"When the Spirit is poured out upon us from on
High"* that *"righteousness will dwell"* (Isa. 32:15-16).

Being a "tree of righteousness" is not to be confused with
trying to do the right thing. This passage is not talking about the
result of human effort, but rather the fruit that is born in us by
the one referred to in 1John 2:1 as *"Jesus Christ, the righteous."*
Philippians 1:11 says that we have been, *"filled with the fruit of*

righteousness that comes through Jesus Christ." As a result of the indwelling presence of the righteous one himself, we have become *"slaves of righteousness"* (Rom. 6:18), because *"a good tree cannot bear bad fruit"* (Matt. 7:18).

In Galatians 5:22-23, Paul refers to the fruit of God's presence in us as *"The fruit of the Spirit."* According to this passage, this "fruit" includes love, joy, peace, patience, kindness, goodness, faithfulness, gentleness and self-control. Each of these qualities and characteristics will be evident and increasing in the life of anyone who is truly born of God, because they are all aspects of God's own "divine nature" which all Christians have *"become partakers of"* (2 Pet. 1:4). As we continue to "abide in him," the life of God's Holy Spirit continues to abide in us, bringing forth the fruit of His holy nature in our thoughts, desires, words and actions.

In Ephesians 5:9, Paul referred to the fruit of God's presence in us as *"The fruit of light."* According to 1 John 1:4, God is Light, so in essence the phrase *"the fruit of light"* is really just another way of saying *"the fruit of God."* Paul goes on to define this "fruit" broadly by saying that it consists of all *"goodness, righteousness and truth."* Goodness, righteousness and truth will all be evident in the life of anyone who is truly born of God. This only makes sense, since God is light, and we are now *"sons of light"* (Luke 12:36, 1 Thess. 5:5).

The clear message of all these passages is that God desires to bear His fruit in our lives through the presence of His Word and Spirit within us. This type of fruit is primarily internal in the form of the changes that take place within us as God replaces the *"old man"* we once were with the *"new man"* we now are in Christ (Col. 3:10). Through the power of His word and Spirit within us, God transforms us into the image and likeness of Jesus, thereby causing His kingdom to come and His will to be done within us.

But God desires not only to see His kingdom come and His will manifest *in* us, but also *through* us, in the lives of others. At

97

some point, the fruit that is born *in* us needs to become fruit that is born *through* us.

For example, at some point, the fruit of love will be expressed, through our words or actions, to someone else. This same thing is true of patience, kindness, goodness, faithfulness, gentleness and righteousness. Ultimately, the fruit that is born inside of us must come out, and throughout the New Testament, there are several ways this is pictured as happening.

The Fruit Of The Kingdom

In Matthew 21:43, Jesus said that the Kingdom of God would be taken away from the Jews and *"given to a people who will produce its fruit."* As the people of God, the Israelites had the privilege and the responsibility of bringing forth the fruit of God's kingdom in the earth. (See Isa. 27:6) But they were not fulfilling this responsibility, so Jesus said the kingdom would be given to someone who would—namely, the church. It is now the privilege and the responsibility of the church to produce the "fruit" of the kingdom, which ultimately consists of anything that helps to establish God's kingdom in people's lives.

The most powerful and obvious fruit of the kingdom is produced whenever the lost come to know Jesus Christ as their Lord and Savior. This was the fruit Jesus referred to in John 4:35-36 when He told his disciples:

> *Open your eyes and look at the fields! They are ripe*
> *for harvest. He who reaps is receiving wages and is*
> *gathering fruit for life eternal.*

And it was this same fruit Jesus referred to in John 15:16, when he told his disciples, *"I chose you, and appointed you that you would go and bear fruit and that your fruit would remain."*

It is important that we understand that winning the lost to Jesus is seldom as easy as simply picking a piece of fruit. The fact is, winning a lost person to Jesus is quite often the work of many people over many years. One person may continually plant the seed of God's word in a friend's heart for many years without seeing any growth. Then, years later sometimes, another Christian may come along and nurture this seed in some way or another, helping to give it ideal growing conditions and cause it to "sprout" into a new life.

Jesus referred to this in John 4:38 when He told His disciples:

> *I sent you to reap that for which you have not laboured; others have laboured, and you have entered into their labour.*

Paul also expressed this concept in 1 Corinthians 3:6, when he said, *"I planted the seed, Apollos watered it, but God made it grow."* Even though we may not be the one to lead someone in the prayer of salvation, we are still producing the "fruit of the kingdom" every time we plant, water, or otherwise nurture the seed of God's word in people's hearts.

While winning the lost to Jesus is without question the foremost external fruit we can produce, it is by no means the only way we can produce the "fruit of the kingdom." Ultimately, we produce the fruit of the kingdom of God whenever we speak His word, share His life, minister His Spirit, and express His love to others.

Certainly, the best example of producing the fruit of the kingdom in its many forms is the ministry of Jesus. Everywhere He went, Jesus proclaimed the Good News of God's kingdom in word and deed—healing the sick, the blind, the deaf and the lame, raising people from the dead, setting captives free, and standing up for the rights of the oppressed.

In John 10:32, Jesus referred to the many miracles that he performed as *"good works."* And in John 14:12, Jesus said that every

Christian would produce this same "fruit" of good works that He produced, and even *"greater works."* Despite what some people think, the church not only has the *ability* to do these things, but the *responsibility* to do them. We are now the ones who have been entrusted with the gospel of the kingdom, and the primary way that God expects the church to produce the "fruit" of the kingdom is by following Jesus' example of going around *"doing good and healing all who are oppressed by the devil"* (Acts 10:38).

Quite early in our marriage, my husband and I realized that God expects us to bear fruit all round. In obedience, we continually abide in the true vine with evident fruits of God in us and the ongoing fruit of the kingdom. Having lived this way over the years, while waiting and after having the miracle children, it has become a way of life for us, and we are diligently teaching our children likewise by role modelling.

Hopes and dreams for the future; such were the thoughts of this newly married man. What will become of my marriage? How will my wife's personality develop in our marriage? How will our future children turn out? These questions do not have immediate answers, nor are they meant to be answered so early on in the journey. The idea is to use these questions to stir up what one values and shape priorities.

Listen to the following words from the Psalmist:

> *Blessed is everyone who fears the Lord, who walks in his ways! You shall eat the fruit of the labour of your hands; you shall be blessed, and it shall be well with you. Your wife will be like a fruitful vine within your house; your children will be like olive shoots around your table. Behold, thus shall the man be blessed who fears the Lord.*

Psalm 128:1-4

This is the scripture from where the title of this book is taken. So, let's attempt to unpack these verses: One of the main points I want to emphasize is how the wife who is described as a fruitful vine and the children as olive shoots are a consequence of the man's lifestyle. For example, Psalm 128:1 pronounces a blessing upon all men and women who fear the Lord and walk in His ways. This is another way of saying that blessed are those who worship God and obey Him.

After the Psalmist declares this universal blessing upon all who worship God and obey Him, he illustrates how this promise bears fruit within the highly specific example of the family unit. The man who worships God for who He is and obeys Him will experience blessing in three areas: in his work, in his marriage to his wife, and in his children's lives (Ps. 128:2-3). These are marvellous promises of God in His word to husbands and fathers everywhere who acknowledge Him for who He is and obey Him.

It is crucial to understand that the Spirit of God, through the Psalmist, blesses all those who fear God and obey Him. Fearing God is more than intellectual acceptance in believing that God is God. It is knowledge of God that may have started in the head, but now that knowledge comes out of the heart in worship and reverence. This is total worship, which means that the head and the heart are working together as one. It seems to me that this is the man in view within Psalm 128 and all men and women who exhibit the same.

Back to the passage, worshiping and obeying God is kind of connected to bringing about blessings in the lives of those who do them. Husbands and fathers are promised success in what their hands have produced (Ps. 128:2).

This means that they will be able to provide for their families. These same men will see an abundance of life in their marriage and in their wives. After all, this seems to be the point behind the image of the fruitful vine (Ps. 128:3a).

Lastly, these men will not have children just to have children. These worshipful and obedient fathers will have children who are olive shoots, which means that they have abundant life in them, like their father (Ps. 128:3b).

Psalm 128:4 states: *"Behold, thus shall the man be blessed who fears the Lord."* This is a clear and simple declaration that the worshipful and obedient man will be blessed. He can be assured of it. The only question to face is whether the man believes God's word. Does he take God and His word at face value? Is the man willing to place all into His hands to see God's work and bless according to His word?

Chapter 10

THREE MIRACLE BABIES! GOD MAKES EVERYTHING BEAUTIFUL IN HIS TIME

In April 2005, my husband and I arrived in Canada as Missionary Intercessors and Foreign Trained Professionals (Chartered Engineer and Experienced Educator, respectively). The Lord used the call of Abraham to epitomize our call as missionaries in Canada. He said the land of Canada is our land of Canaan; He assured us that He would raise prophetic helping hands for us and that we would have our children there.

Three months after, God Almighty, the Master planner, directed Women Intercessors for the Church and the Nations (Wailing Women Worldwide), to raise intercessors in Canada. In July 2005, three of the International Coordinators of Wailing Women came to Canada on our 10th wedding anniversary. The team spent time praying for my husband and me and the Lord confirmed His words again. We birthed the manifestation of our children through fervent fasting, prayer and declarations of the Word of God.

We consulted a specialist gynaecologist shortly after we arrived in Canada. The first miracle was that we had free medical coverage in Canada. After consultations with renowned gynaecologists and subsequent thorough medical examinations, results showed that I had uterine fibroids and my husband had oligospermia which refers to semen with a low concentration of sperm, commonly found in male infertility. Often, semen with a decreased sperm concentration may also show significant abnormalities in sperm morphology and motility. So, he was referred to a urologist and the wait list was almost six months.

My gynaecologist did further investigations to see if my fallopian tubes were clear or blocked. One thing remarkable in our experience was that we saturated every single medical report with prayers. We rejected what was not in alignment with the Word of God; we spoke into existence the Word of God concerning fruitfulness. We prayed earnestly asking the Lord to anoint just one sperm and send it on assignment to fertilize the right egg and start the process of divine procreation; I was that specific. We spoke to my uterus, calling the power of the Most High to overshadow it the same way the Holy Spirit came upon Mary, the mother of Jesus Christ. The medical results enabled us to pray specific prayer points, knowing that at the name of Jesus every knee must bow including "oligospermia" and "uterine fibroids".

Our First Miracle Baby

Exactly ten years after our wedding, the Lord miraculously touched my womb. We did an intensive twenty-one-day fasting and prayer with the theme, Prayer for Supernatural Conception and Divine Protection, as recommended by a trusted and anointed servant of God in 2005. We prayed fervently every day. The enemy tried to use distraction to hinder the purpose of God's divine appointment, but the Grace of God enabled us to triumph over all the devices of the wicked. It was indeed real spiritual warfare. The devil tried to use little provocations to distract the purpose of God for us. My husband and I would disagree over nothing. Thank God we recognized the tricks of the devil and overcame him by the blood of the Lamb and by the Word of our testimony. Within the twenty-one days of fasting, I conceived without having any idea.

Weeks passed, and I began to feel sick. I visited the doctor who, at first, thought I had the flu. My doctor decided to do a pregnancy test and it was positive. I looked at my husband and tears rolled down my cheeks—tears of joy.

When the Lord restored the fortunes of Zion, we were like those who dreamed. Our mouths were filled with laughter, our tongues with songs of joy.

Psalm 126:1-2

It was one of the best days of my life. I closed my eyes in awe of the Lord. I didn't mind the presence of the doctor; the tears kept flowing uncontrollably out of my eyes as my husband began to talk to the Indian doctor about our experience. We left the clinic, glorifying the Lord, praising and worshipping His Majesty for who He is.

The next day, we headed straight to the specialist gynaecologist's office. When he saw us, he talked about all our urology appointment and all the tests and investigations for me. My husband could not help but break the news to him. He was shocked to hear the news; however, we gave him the test results from the doctor. He said, "I don't get this." He quickly gave us a requisition to go for an ultrasound to confirm what we were saying. We drove straight to the ultrasound clinic, and in a few minutes, I was watching my baby on the ultrasound screen, listening to her heartbeat. It was so beautiful, emotional and wonderful. We returned with the results to the gynaecologist and again he asked us what happened; we told him that God had done it for us through prayer. Right away, the gynaecologist transferred my name from the infertility list to the prenatal list as he was also an obstetrician! We continued praying every day over the baby in the womb.

My Daily Prayer And Declarations

The Lord shall perfect everything concerning me. The Lord who has started His good work of creation in me will complete it.

Philippians 1:6

By the power in the blood of the Lord Jesus Christ, I confess that my pregnancy is perfect, in the name of Jesus. Every part of my body shall function properly for the formation of the baby, in Jesus's name, and my blood shall circulate effectively. Everything that passes from me to the baby for its development shall be healthy, in Jesus's name. I confess that I am strong; weakness is not my lot, in the name of Jesus.

I reject cramps, varicose veins, piles, backaches, vomiting, constipation, anaemia, vitamin and mineral deficiencies, swollen hands and feet, hypertension, convulsion and diabetes, in the name of Jesus. My urine shall remain normal, in the name of Jesus (Ps. 3-5). The activities of eaters of flesh and drinkers of blood will not prosper in my life, in the name of Jesus. I refuse and reject all negative dreams, visions, prophecies and imaginations, in the name of Jesus.

I confess God's Word in Exodus 23:26, that I shall not have a miscarriage, abnormal bleeding or malformation of the baby, in Jesus' name. I shall be a joyous mother of children. My womb is fruitful. My children shall be like olive plants round about our table. Every aspect of the growth, formation and development of my baby shall be perfect, in Jesus' name.

I shall not have nausea, irritation, headache, internal or external pain. I declare that by the stripes of Jesus, I am healed. I shall tread upon sickness and all the powers of the devil. My body is the temple of the Holy Spirit. I have the life and health of Christ in me. The Sun of righteousness has arisen over me, having conquered sickness, pains and Satan. God's will for me and my baby is to prosper and be in good health. God is at work in me right now. His blood is flowing in me and perfecting all that pertains to my baby's formation in Jesus's name.

I declare that every disease and germ should die now, in Jesus' name. Nothing shall harm me or my baby, in Jesus' name, because

the Bible says that, "If I drink any deadly thing, it shall not harm me." I confess that as I go to deliver my baby, the Lord shall direct those taking the delivery on what care suits me and my baby, in Jesus' name.

My pregnancy is established in righteousness. I am far from oppression. Therefore, I shall not fear, no terror shall come near me, no evil shall befall my baby, and no plague shall come near my dwelling place.

As the pregnancy progresses, the Lord shall fulfill the number of my days. I shall not have a premature baby; my baby shall come out alive, strong and healthy. My pelvis is wide enough to allow my baby to pass through, in Jesus name.

According to Isaiah 43, I confess that when I pass through the water, the Lord will be with me; if through the rivers, it shall not overflow me; and if I walk through the fire, I shall neither be burnt, nor shall the flame scourge me. I shall give birth without pain, in Jesus' name. The Lord shall take away from me every sickness of pregnancy and I am not afraid, because I have been redeemed from the curse of bringing forth in agony in Jesus' name (Gal. 4).

I boldly confess Isaiah 66:7 that, before I travail, I will give

birth. According to 1 Timothy 2:15, I will be saved in childbearing because I am walking in faith, love, holiness, and self-control.

According to Psalm 118:17; neither I nor my baby will die. We shall both live to declare the works of the Lord, in Jesus' name. My cervix shall be fully dilated, and the passage big and open enough for the baby to pass through with ease. The delivery shall be perfect, in Jesus' name. No evil shall befall me or my baby. No weapon of the devil that is fashioned against me or my baby shall prosper, in Jesus' name.

The Lord is the strength of my life, of whom shall I be afraid? He is my Deliverer, my God, my Buckler and the Horn of my sal-

vation. The Lord is all I need. He shall strengthen the bars of my gate. He has blessed the children within me. Therefore, I shall do valiantly. By the grace of God, I will live to be a happy mother. I refuse prolonged labour and reject all pains from the devil during labour and afterwards.

My children shall grow up to know and love the Lord; the Lord shall supply all our needs during pregnancy and after delivery, in Jesus' name.

The Appointment With The Urologist

Glory to the name of the Lord, because I shall have what I say, in Jesus' name. When I was a little over two months along in pregnancy, we honored the appointment date with the urologist for some reason. As we got there, the urologist wanted to begin diagnosing, but my husband, with joy and excitement, announced to him that I was pregnant already. Again, he was shocked and confused because, according to medical diagnosis, my husband had oligospermia. He began to testify to the powerful, miraculous and sovereign God whom we serve and what He had done for us regarding this conception.

1 Peter 5:8 says:

Be alert and of sober mind. Your enemy the devil prowls around like a roaring lion looking for someone to devour.

About four months along in the pregnancy, I tripped while having a bath in the bathtub and fell on my side. I called upon

Jesus, prayed, and I headed straight to work. By the end of the workday, the pain was unbearable, so I ended up in the hospital Emergency Department (ER). The ER doctor examined me and left. He returned and wheeled me to the x-ray department and left me at the door. I laid there on the stretcher in the most excruciating pain you can ever imagine, calling upon my God, the Great Healer, to cover my baby and myself with the blood of Jesus. I also asked the Lord for deliverance, protection and healing.

I was very close to the nursing station, so one of the nurses rushed to me and said that I should not consent to the x-ray as it was not proper to have an x-ray during pregnancy, and she left quickly like an angel. Shortly after, the said ER doctor. reappeared and I said to him, "Why are you sending me for x-rays? Don't you realize that I'm pregnant?"

The doctor threw a tantrum; he became very angry and visibly shook. He began to yell at me, saying that I must get the x-ray. I quietly said to him, I will not sign the paperwork to consent for this x-ray as it is not safe, and I don't want to harm my baby. He walked away in a fit of anger and left me there.

After a while, the nurses came back to reassure me not to give in. Of course, at that point, I had started praying even more fervently. When the doctor returned, he moved me back to the room and began to say all sorts of things. I refused to react negatively as I had figured out that the devil wanted to use the doctor to harm my child. He angrily wrote a prescription and stormed out of my room, leaving the prescription there. I got dressed, took the prescription for courtesy, and left.

Our house was just a few minutes away, so I walked home crying to my God to heal me. After we filled the prescription, it was boldly written on the bottle, "Do not take if you are pregnant or breastfeeding." When I saw this, regardless of the money that we paid to fill the prescription, I did not take that medication. Again, I chose to bear the pain and trust my God to heal me. To the glory of

God, He healed me of my disease and delivered me from destruction (Ps. 107:20).

I had a vision of The Lord Jesus Christ looking so gracious and dazzling. He came to me and touched me, and I woke up totally well. The pain was completely gone.

The Fibroid Result

One of the ultrasound scans that I had during the pregnancy, showed multiple uterine fibroids; one of the fibroids was about 13 cm long. I remember how unprofessional the radiologists were. According professional practice, they should not tell the patient

their findings but send the ultrasound results to the doctor who made the requisition. It is the duty of the doctor to tell the patient and explain things at a follow-up appointment.

For some inexplicable reason, this radiologist began to make sarcastic comments about the numerous fibroids in my womb. *"Where did you get all these fibroids from?"* I totally ignored him and continued to speak the Word of the Lord commanding the fibroids to shrink and allow my baby to develop perfectly. To the glory of my heavenly Father, the one that has the final say in every situation, at full term, my baby was born.

My Vow To The Lord

I had the most remarkable childbirth, by the supernatural power of the Highest God; I had my baby without an epidural, episiotomy, or any other medications. My obstetrician, the nurse that took care of me and everyone else testified that the delivery was remarkably different. My first miracle baby weighed 10.8 pounds (4.899kg) at birth. Obviously, God wanted to demonstrate that He had the final authority regarding the life and development of the baby in my womb.

Over the years as a Christian, I've observed believers in Christ pray desperately when they need God to give them children, and once they get pregnant, they give excuses as to why they are no longer active in church or even serving the Lord as they used to do. I am quite aware of the hormonal changes that a woman's body experiences during pregnancy and how that can potentially slow her down. However, I believe Christians should continue fervently in the Lord and in His service in pregnancy. That is where the grace of God comes to play. I do not agree that the blessings of God should be used as an excuse to backslide or get complacent.

I made a vow to the Lord, to continue being committed, dedicated, consecrated, fervent, zealous and passionate in my love and service to Him. God honoured my heart's desires, throughout my first pregnancy; I was fully involved in advancing the Kingdom of God. I attended vigils every week until the week before my delivery. Actually, the brethren were literally pleading with me to stop coming to the vigils as they were scared that I might give birth right there. It will always be a pleasure to serve my God.

Our Second Miracle Baby

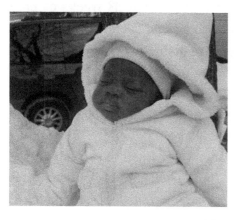

While waiting on the Lord for my children, I would always pray to have them back-to-back. At some point, the Lord said to me that someday I would pray that I do not want any more children. That was quite unbelievable, unimaginable, unrealistic and far-fetched. Dear friends, God Almighty honoured my heart's desires. While I was pregnant with my first baby, the Lord revealed to me that the second baby would come right after. Exactly eight months after I had the first baby, God visited me again and I conceived my second baby. The day I had the pregnancy test, the doctor asked me if I wanted to keep it. I thought that was a ridiculous and ungodly question, and I responded, *"Of course this is a miracle for me."*

The cost of giving birth in Canada was an average of $10,000 for those who did not have health insurance; but as a Canadian, I paid nothing and had a year of paid maternity leave to take care of each of my babies. It could only be God Almighty. The Master planner worked everything out for us; we did not spend a dollar during my pregnancy and all our children are Canadian citizens by birth. Indeed, in His time, He makes all things beautiful (Eccles. 3:11). I continued declaring the scriptures and prayers on supernatural conception and divine protection over my baby in the womb as usual.

The Glucose Screening

A glucose screening, which is a routine test during pregnancy that checks a pregnant woman's blood glucose (sugar) level, was booked. I had the test done between 24 and 28 weeks of pregnancy. The result showed that I had gestational diabetes, which is high blood sugar. Like other types of diabetes, gestational diabetes affects your cells' use of sugar (glucose). It causes high blood sugar that can affect your pregnancy and your baby's health. So, I was given a certain dose of insulin on a daily basis to regulate my blood sugar while watching my calorie intake very closely.

I was sent for an orientation course. I had to self-administer the daily insulin. I cried to the Lord to help me, and of course, He did, as usual. Though it was very tough for me, by the grace of

Almighty God, I stood upon the promises of the Word of God and trusted Him to do a miracle again in my life. My husband and I, in agreement, continued to speak the Word of the Lord to my body, to the baby in the womb and believed God for another miracle. The Sovereign Lord kept me healthy and strong to carry the pregnancy successfully, while looking after my toddler, working part-time and carrying out the work of His Kingdom diligently.

I hosted national conferences in Canada; I attended conferences in America; we carried out very sensitive national assignments to the different cities of Canada; we did road trips, prophetic work, reached out to so many people in need, etc. I continued in love, faith and speaking the Word of God to the baby in the womb, telling God the specific birth weight I wanted and claiming my healing. God granted me all my heart's desires. At the fullness of time, God defied gestational diabetes and delivered into our hands the most beautiful, precious, fearfully and wonderfully made baby, weighing exactly 8.3 pounds as I decreed. 1 Timothy 2:15 says:

> *But women will be saved through childbearing if they continue in faith, love and holiness with propriety.*

Blessed To Be A Blessing

God Almighty, anointed me and my husband with a specific grace to pray for those who are waiting on the Lord for their miracle children. Personally, my heart deeply goes out to such ladies. I pray for them with compassion, having walked that road myself. It doesn't matter who the individual is, as long as they have such need, I connect to their need automatically and stand in the gap for them. When the Lord makes the opportunity available, I joyfully share a little bit of my experience to help build their faith in God. God provided such a platform the same month I had my second baby.

Two weeks before I was due, we organized the inauguration of our ministry in Mississauga, Ontario, Canada. We invited a couple we met at the employment resource centre like everybody else. Thank God they honoured the invitation without knowing that God had a plan to break the yoke of eighteen years of barrenness in their lives. At the height of ministering, my husband called out the lady under the unction of the Holy Spirit and prayed for the fruit of the womb. She was reluctant and kind of embarrassed, but she came out anyway. I began to pray in the spirit and in tongues. The power of God came down mightily upon the sister and she fell on the floor under the anointing of the Holy Spirit. After the prayer, we scheduled a one-on-one to follow up counselling for the couple.

The following week, behold, the Lord delivered into my hands another beautiful miracle baby girl. So, this couple came to visit us after the birth of the baby. I took this lady aside, shared passionately from my heart more specific details about my supernatural childbirth experiences and numerous praise reports. I had my few days old baby in my hands and I began to minister to her with great faith. I gave her some of my books that I used, such as, *Destroying the Yoke of Barrenness,* by Dr. D. K. Olukoya, and a copy of *Supernatural Childbirth* by Jackie Mize. I also gave her the exact copy of the twenty-one-day fast that my husband and I embarked upon just before I conceived my first miracle baby.

I encouraged her strongly to talk to her husband and work in agreement so that they could decide when to begin the twenty-one-day fast. I must say, the Lord used me to open the woman's spiritual eyes to realize that it is her right as a child of God to bring forth a baby according to the Word of the Lord.

According to her, she left my house with so much faith, ready to confront and overcome all hindrances opposing God's promise of childbearing for her. She and her husband went home and followed every single direction and began the twenty-one-day fast. She read all the books, made all the declarations; and that month of January, she conceived. Over eighteen years of barrenness was broken, and in the month of October 2008, she gave birth to a baby boy. That boy turned ten years old in 2018.

Our Third Miracle Baby

My husband and I began to pray to the Lord once again for a male child whose name, God had revealed to me twelve years ago,

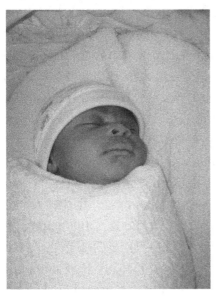

before he was born. In order to demonstrate my unwavering faith in the promise of God, I decided to use his name as my email password. I made an agreement with God that I will only change the password when he was born; that was exactly what I did. Our two little angels joined us in the prayer. We were very specific. According to the time of life, in His own miraculous way again, I conceived. I was so excited that I went to my doctor to do a urine test for me. He did, and surely, I was pregnant. We continued speaking the Word to the baby.

I was now five years older than when I'd had my first baby. The very first routine blood work I did in the first trimester showed a very big danger and had "red flag" stamped on it: Trisomy 23. Trisomy 23 is a chromosome disorder which is caused by an alteration in the number or genetic structure of chromosomes. Trisomy ('three bodies') means the affected person has forty-seven chromosomes instead of forty-sex. Down syndrome, Edward syndrome and Patau syndrome are the most common forms of Trisomy. Children affected by Trisomy usually have a range of birth defects, including delayed development and intellectual disabilities.

The medical professional team advised me strongly to terminate the pregnancy, but of course, that was not an option as I choose to trust my God who has done it twice for me. I returned from the doctor's office with the Trisomy 23 result and I went straight down on my face and wept before the Lord. I reiterated to the Lord our covenant. I reflected on James 1:17-18:

> *Every good thing given and every perfect gift is from above; it comes down from the Father of lights [the Creator and Sustainer of the heavens], in whom there is no variation [no rising or setting] or shadow cast by His turning [for He is perfect and never changes]. It was of His own will that He gave us birth [as His children] by the word of truth, so that we would be a kind of first fruits of His creatures [a prime example of what* He created to be set apart to Himself—*sanctified, made holy for His divine purposes]*. **(AMP)**

I was referred to a genetics specialist who was to enlighten me about amniocentesis—a highly-invasive procedure—where a sample of the amniotic fluid is taken from the foetus and examined.

The specialist explained the risk of possible needle injury to the baby, outright miscarriage and the fact that even if they were to discover any genetic disorder, there was no medical solution. Again, I trusted God to prove His Sovereignty, because it was an opportunity to witness to the specialist about the miraculous and ultimate power of the Most High God. I walked away from that appointment, glorifying God in advance.

In June 2011, the pregnancy was about six months along and I was at a national conference. Without mentioning this situation to anybody except my husband, the "Sovereign Lord" called me out through a word of prophecy. He gave specific instructions regarding the baby in my womb and what needed to be done to secure his life

from the evil plot of the devil. I laid on my face in awe and reverence to this, my God, just worshipping Him in tears. I promptly obeyed God's instructions. I knew right there and then that it was settled. On my next prenatal appointment, I told my doctors not to engage me in any discussion about the so-called Trisomy 23 anymore; of course, they respected my decision.

While I was in labour, I worshipped God all through as my nurses and doctor were checking on the baby and me. When he was

born, it was glorious to see my wonderfully and fearfully made son from the throne room of God, the Creator. The specialists gathered in my room quickly, and after examining him thoroughly using different medical pieces of equipment, the chief obstetrician consultant said to me, *"He is perfect."*

I responded, *"Thank you."*

He replied, *"Thank your God."* He obviously figured that we believe in God.

Chapter 11
WHO IS A TRUE MOTHER?

Motherhood is a noble task and a divine call. Most mothers see it as a natural thing. I believe strongly that motherhood is more spiritual. It takes abiding in Jesus Christ and allowing our Heavenly Father the Vinedresser to groom you continually until you bear good fruits that can bless the world. Parenting is a lifetime responsibility; once you enroll, you do not graduate until death. You must be engaged, physically, emotionally, financially, psychologically and mentally as a mother.

According to Deuteronomy 6:6-7, being a mother involves interacting, discussing, thinking and processing life. You must always rely solely on the help of the Holy Spirit at every point in time. People who do not know the Holy Spirit use terms like *'my gut feeling,' 'something told me' 'I don't know what it is, but I just felt...'* None of these is the authentic manifestation of the true Spirit of God.

Characteristics Of A True Mother

Holy Spirit Controlled

In order to please God as a Mom, you need the indwelling of the Holy Spirit. One can receive the Holy Spirit in measures by being totally immersed to manifest His fruits with other people daily in our life.

The fruit of the Holy Spirit is love, joy, peace, patience, kindness, goodness, faithfulness, gentleness and self-control. The Holy Spirit has to be your consultant, best friend, confidant and senior partner. It is amazing how the Holy Spirit reminds us of things. Countless times I've misplaced something precious and the Holy Spirit will just lead me to the right spot where I kept it. He covers my blind spot when I am unguarded. He reveals the hidden things of the devil and the areas where our children struggle. He is our Teacher, Guide, Helper and Strength.

Full Of Grace

A true Mom should have an overflowing grace of God, which enables her to meet divine standards of parenting. Only the grace of God can carry you through the ups and downs of parenting. The fact that God has given you a miracle child does not mean there will be no challenges; actually, tough times will Come, but you will overcome by His grace that is made sufficient.

A Fountain Of Love

This is *agape* or the love of God; it is unconditional love. The Bible says that God is love. Human love is an intense affection for another person that is based on feelings and can change at any given moment, but *agape* love is unconditional; it is based on God's nature. God's nature is consistent, and so is His love for us.

The best example of the nature of God's love is the story of The Prodigal Son. The father's love did not change, even though his son left home, wasted his wealth, and ended up destitute. When he saw his son returning home, he ran to him and hugged him; that showed that he never stopped loving him. As Christian mothers, we can only give God's kind of love once we have received it ourselves.

Allowing God To Love You

You cannot give to others what you do not have; before you can give God's love to others, you must be indwelt by God's love. 1 John 4:9-15 says:

> *This is how God showed His love among us: He sent His one and only Son into the world that we might live through Him. This is love: not that we loved God, but that He loved us and sent His Son as an atoning sacrifice for our sins. Dear friends, since God so loved us, we also ought to love one another. No one has ever seen God; but if we love one another, God lives in us and His love is made complete in us. This is how we know that we live in him and him in us: He has given us of His Spirit. And we have seen and testify that the Father has sent His Son to be the Savior of the world. If anyone acknowledges that Jesus is the Son of God, God lives in them and they in God.*

To be indwelt by God's love, you need to first understand that God loves you. He loves you so much that He gave you the ultimate gift, His only begotten Son. Jesus laid down His life to pay for your sins, even though He knew that you did not deserve it. In our rebellion, God still sent Jesus to die for us.

This is too good to be true, but it really is, and no one else can ever love you this way. You should personally agree with God that Jesus is your Saviour. Confess that Jesus is the Son of God. Some people do this by talking to God silently; others confess Jesus as their Lord by talking to God aloud. Some people do this alone; others do it publicly. However, what matters is that you personally tell God that you agree with Him, that Jesus is your Saviour.

When you confess that Jesus is your Saviour, He sends His Spirit to dwell in you. He becomes your loving Father and you become His beloved child. The Holy Spirit enables you to feel His love. This is why people who recently received Christ are excited; they've experienced the greatest love, peace and joy ever. Are you indwelt by God's love? Is God's Spirit resident in you? Have you confessed to God that Jesus is your Saviour? Can you make peace with God today?

Draw Continually From God's Love

It is not enough to be indwelt by God's love; you also must continually draw from the love of God.

> *[16]We have come to know [by personal observation and experience], and have believed [with deep, consistent faith] the love which God has for us. God is love, and the one who abides in love abides in God, and God abides continually in him. [17]In this [union and fellowship with Him], love is completed and perfected with us, so that we may have confidence in the day of Judgment [with assurance and boldness to face Him]; because as He is, so are we in this world.*

1 John 4: 16-17 (AMP)

Our understanding and appreciation of God's love for us should be ever fresh and increasing. God's love is like a fine diamond; a multi-faceted wonder of brilliance, depth and clarity. We should keep discovering new depths, or facets, of God's love.

Some Ways To Grow In The Knowledge Of God's Love

Prayerfully Reflect On The Scripture About God's Love

Ask God to open the eyes of your heart to know and understand His love. Apostle Paul, speaking to Ephesians said:

> *So that Christ may dwell in your hearts through your faith, And may you, having been [deeply] rooted and [securely] grounded in love, be fully capable of comprehending with all the saints (God's people) the width and length and height and depth of His love [fully experiencing that amazing, endless love]; and [that you may come] to know [practically, through personal experience] the love of Christ which far surpasses [mere] knowledge [without experience], that you may be filled up [throughout your being] to all the fullness of God [so that you may have the richest experience of God's presence in your lives, completely filled and flooded with God Himself].*

> **Ephesians 3:17-19 (AMP)**

Rely On The Love Of God

As you learn more about God's love, He provides you with many personal and practical ways to rely on His love. Making a resolve to rely on His love increases your confidence in Him. You rely on God's love by choosing to draw near to Him, especially when you are unworthy.

There is no fear in love [dread does not exist]. But perfect (complete, full-grown) love drives out fear, because fear involves [the expectation of divine] punishment, so the one who is afraid [of God's judgment] is not perfected in love [has not grown into a sufficient understanding of God's love].

1 John 4:18 AMP

We tend to make our performance the basis for entering into God's presence. God says we are not worthy to come into His presence on the basis of what we do for Him, but only on the basis of what Jesus has done for us.

Choose To Let His People Love You

You must allow God's love to help your weakness rather than stay aloof. Drawing near to God is not enough, you need to get involved with other Christians.

Always Thank God For His Love

A thankful heart, especially in painful circumstances, shows that we love God. Psalm 34:1 should be our daily lifestyle: *"I will bless the LORD at all times: His praise shall continually be in my mouth."* Count your blessings and name them, personally thank God for blessing you daily.

Love Others

Give the love of God to others always. This may sound contradictory, but it is super rewarding and empowering. Withholding God's love from others shows that you do not trust Him. It is only selfish Christians who are never excited about God's love. God's love refreshes the soul; it increases our capacity to receive and appreciate Him.

Be An Embodiment Of Solution

Jesus Christ said in John 16:33:

> *I have told you these things so that in me you may have peace. In this world you will have trouble. But take heart! I have overcome the world.*

Be A Wise Builder

James 3:17 says:

> *But the wisdom that is from above is first pure, then peaceable, gentle, and easy to be entreated, full of mercy and good fruits, without partiality, and without hypocrisy.*

Moms are called to wisely build their children, recognizing that each child is unique and beautifully created by God. We should relate to our children equally. Naturally, we tend to gravitate toward the child that is always obedient, compliant, outstanding and pleases us in every way. However, the true test of a godly mother, is the ability to build up all her children and love the stubborn child.

Model The Life Of Integrity

Live out the message that you preach. Be a good role model for your children. Timothy is a typical example. 2 Timothy 1:5 says:

I *am reminded of your sincere faith, which first
lived in your grandmother Lois and in your mother
Eunice and, I am persuaded, now lives in you also.*

Lois and Eunice are examples of the powerful influence a
mother and grandmother can have on children. Let your children
testify that you took them to church and taught them how to pray
and study the Word of God. Paul recognized Lois and Eunice's con-
tributions when women were rarely mentioned in church. He honoured their impact on the life of Timothy, who eventually became
the pastor of the church at Ephesus. Christian mothers should know
that their godly influence has an eternal impact on the lives and
futures of their children and grandchildren.

Be Prayerful

You should press closer to God in prayer; it makes you know
Him better, understand His ways deeper and follow Him closer.
Continue to build your "prayer muscle" and rejoice that God hears
you and delights in you to accomplish His kingdom purposes.

A praying mother must be humble. She should put away unforgiveness, sin, and bitterness to avoid grieving the Spirit of God
(Eph. 4:30). She must also understand her stand before God.

Be An Intercessor

Intercession is prayer or pleading for the needs of others,
nations, or institutions. Intercession involves refusing to let go until
God's promise and will are fulfilled in your life.

Intercession is the key to achieving God's plan for your life.
You must realize that you are not fighting against humans, but
against forces, authorities, rulers of darkness, and spiritual powers
in the heavenly places (Eph. 6:12).

The Battle Plan

Every child of God has the direct line or address of God. You can boldly come into His presence anytime (Heb. 4:16) and enjoy free access to God. In God's presence, you can discover His battle plan for that situation in your life and target your prayers rightly. It is called battle strategy or precision prayer. Ask God for wisdom and it will be given to you (James 1:5). Let God change your heart so that you will know how to think and do only things that please Him.

Armed For Battle

The weapons of our warfare are not carnal. Intercessory prayer is a serious matter; just like soldiers preparing for battle, we cannot defeat the enemy without our heavenly weapons. We must go into "battle" armed and equipped spiritually (2 Cor. 10:3-4).

Put On The Amour

Recognize that Jesus is in control of your situations and your entire household. Jesus rules over forces, authorities, powers, rulers and over all creatures and creation, in the present and in the future. (Eph. 1:21). He is King of kings and Lord of lords. The weapons of our warfare are not carnal, they are mighty through God to the pulling down of strongholds (2 Cor. 10:3-4) and protect you from enemy attacks.

Bind the Enemy

Bind the work of Satan. Jesus has given you authority to defeat the power of your enemy (Luke 10:19). Take authority over every identified stronghold in the name of Jesus. Always remember that *"the Holy Spirit in you is more powerful that the one that is in the world"* (1 John 4:4).

Jesus is Interceding for You

Take comfort knowing that you are not alone on that battle field; Jesus Christ is interceding on your behalf. The Bible says that Jesus *"is able to save forever those who draw near to God through Him; He always lives to make intercession for them"* (Heb. 7:25).

Persisting in Battle

Intercessory prayer endures all setbacks and overcomes every obstacle. It is prayer that *"presses on"* until we *"apprehend"* God's will in that situation we are facing (Phil. 3:12). This kind of prayer provokes breakthroughs in your life and in the lives of those around you.

Jesus told a story of the persistent friend; who kept knocking on his neighbour's door at midnight for loaves of bread. The neighbour refused to get up, but, "because of his friend's persistence he got up and gave him as much as he needed" (Luke 11:8). After the story, Jesus said,

> *Everyone who asks will receive, everyone who searches will find, and the door will be opened for everyone who knocks.*

Luke 11:10

Therefore, keep asking, keep seeking, keep knocking; in God's time, you shall reap the harvest of your persistence in intercessory prayer.

World Changer

A "world changer" is someone who is radically and passionately devoted to Jesus Christ; he is compassionate towards people and willing to risk everything for the sake of Christ's Kingdom.

It requires sacrifice to be world changers. We cannot give what we do not have; we cannot raise world changers if we are not changing the world. We must assess with honesty our devotion to Christ and His Kingdom. Allow God to build in you what you desire to build into your children. Here are some key points to note for any mother who truly desires to pass on a powerful and godly legacy to her children.

Recreating Who We Are - Keys To Raising Godly Children

Rest on the Grace of God

James 4:6 says, "...He gives us more grace." That is why Scripture says: *"God opposes the proud but shows favour to the humble."* God's grace should be the foundation of your family relationships; always be quick to apologize to your children when you blow it.

Spend Time in the Word, Prayer and Worship

> *"You shall teach them diligently to your children and shall talk of them when you sit in your house, and when you walk by the way, and when you lie down, and when you rise up."*

Deuteronomy 6:7

You can do this in both planned times and unplanned times. I always counted it a privilege to put my children to sleep at night. We would read the Bible, discuss it and pray with them.

Have Your Children Spend Time Alone with Jesus Christ

Our children should have personal, quiet time to pray, read the Bible and meditate on it. Create quiet time for each of them without any electronic devices like iPads, smartphones, tablets, PCs, laptops, TV, or access to any form of social media. They focus on listening to the Lord and developing love and intimacy from His presence alone. Over time, this routine shall become a way of life for each of them.

Stand for the Truth, Even Though You Are Standing Alone

As a believer, it is likely that at some point in your life, you will be challenged to stand alone. You will be in a situation that forces you to choose whether you will obey God or "*follow the crowd.*" Your decision will either glorify God or give the enemies of God an opportunity to scorn Him (2 Sam. 12:14).

A Biblical Example Of Standing Alone

The life of Daniel provides an outstanding example of one who stood alone. When faced with the choice to either forsake his allegiance to the Lord or be thrown into a lions' den, he chose to face the lions. Daniel was willing to die for the sake of God. Daniel remained faithful to God and so he was thrown into the lions' den. God sent an angel to shut the lions' mouths and Daniel was not harmed in any way as a result of his willingness to stand alone.

When King Darius witnessed the mighty power of God that protected Daniel, he wrote this decree:

*In every dominion of my kingdom men [must]
tremble and fear before the God of Daniel: for he
is the living God, and steadfast forever, and his
kingdom that which shall not be destroyed, and his
dominion shall be even unto the end. He delivereth
and rescueth; and he worketh signs and wonders
in heaven and in earth, who hath delivered Daniel
from the power of the lions.*

Daniel 6:26–27

God not only rescued Daniel from destruction, but He prospered
him. The scriptures describe Daniel as a *"man greatly beloved"* by
God and a man with *"an excellent spirit"* (See Dan. 6:3, 10:11).

God is looking for Daniels—men and women who will understand the truths of Scripture and propose to uphold and obey them,
regardless of the cost. When you stand alone, you greatly influence others and bring glory to God. I sincerely appreciate my
Heavenly Father for the diverse opportunities that He gave me
to stand alone at different times and stages of my walk with Him.
Although, some of these moments were unpleasant, like Daniel, I
came out victorious.

Courageous Through Confidence in God

Standing alone requires courage. Courage is not the absence of
fear, but rather a decision to be confident in something or someone
greater than the emotion of fear. To stand alone, you must have confidence in God and obey God and His law. Develop an inner assurance in God even by standing for the truth. My six-year-old child,
by the grace of God, is gradually learning from me. He will boldly
opt out from any class activity that is contrary to the Word of God.

Willingness to Suffer Rejection or Persecution

Please note that it is not everybody who stands alone who always experiences miraculous interventions, like Daniel and his three friends, who chose to die rather than worship a false god. They made a costly decision to uphold righteousness and reject wickedness.

We must Count the Cost

Hebrews 11 gives an account of many heroes of faith who stood alone. Although many of them experienced miraculous deliverance, there were also many who suffered, became *"destitute, afflicted, tormented"* (Heb. 11:37), and eventually died because of horrible torture (Heb. 11:36-40).When you choose to obey God regardless of the cost, you must turn to God for the grace and strength to face the torment and afflictions (Jer. 7:23).

Use the Sword of the Spirit to Wage War Against the Devil

God's Word is the Truth and the believer's most powerful weapon against evil. The Apostle Paul admonishes us to:

> *Be strong in the Lord, and in the power of his might. Put on the whole armor of God that ye may be able to stand against the wiles of the devil. ... Stand therefore, having your loins girt about with truth... And take ... the sword of the Spirit, which is the word of God.*

Ephesians 6:10–11, 14, 17

When Satan tempted Jesus in the wilderness, Christ defeated him by quoting truths from the scriptures. In His response to the devil's first temptation, Jesus emphasized the necessity of knowing God's Word, pointing out that our need for God's Word is just as critical as our need for physical sustenance. He said: *"It is written, Man shall not live by bread alone, but by every word that proceedeth out of the mouth of God"* (Matt. 4:4). We must *know* the truth before we can *stand alone* for truth and defend it.

When given the opportunity to stand alone for Christ, God provides you with the courage and wisdom you need. He has always done the same for me. As the Lord daily guides you in paths of righteousness, for His sake, it is important to:

- Let the Lord renew your mind with the truths of His Word: This will enable you to see life in a perspective that is pleasing to Him (Rom. 12:2).
- Apply God's truth to every aspect of your life and obey the promptings of His Holy Spirit (Ps. 119:105).
- Walk in the strength of the Lord as you identify with Christ's death, burial and resurrection (Rom. 6–8).
- Love the Lord with all your heart and be more concerned about bringing Him honour than with pleasing yourself (John 14:2).
- Realize that you are never alone because God will never leave you nor forsake you (Matt. 28:20).
- Know that when we face persecution, God's grace is sufficient (Matt. 6:11-12).
- Walk in humility before God and man (James 4:6, 10).
- Hate evil and do not yield to the temptation to accept evil gifts (Rom. 2:1).

As we take a stand for God, whatever the cost, His Kingdom shall be advanced. King David's proclamation in Psalm 56:10-13 can be activated:

> *...God is for me. In God will I praise his word: in the Lord will I praise his word. In God have I put my trust: I will not be afraid what man can do unto me. ... Thou hast delivered my soul from death: wilt not thou deliver my feet from falling, that I may walk before God in the light of the living?*

Know That They Are Created for a High Purpose

Everyone has a purpose for being created by the Lord, but not all of us have realized it. When we do not have an accurate understanding of our identity, we either strive to be something we are not or compare ourselves to others.

When we criticize and compete with others to be relevant, thereby being insecure, oversensitive, frustrated and unfulfilled. Competition makes us try too hard to ensure that life happens the way we think it is supposed to.

God doesn't want such for His children. He wants you to have a clear vision for your life. He wants to reveal your gifts and talents, and to show you how to best develop and use them for His glory. God knows that you can only find total fulfillment when you are doing what He created you to do.

About King David, the Bible says that:

> *For after David had served by the counsel of God in his own generation, he fell asleep, was buried with his fathers, and saw decay.*

Acts 13:36

Constantly encourage your children to pursue God's purposes; graciously help them extract "self" from their visions of the Kingdom. Teach them how to inquire of the Lord about their lives, destinies and divine purposes. God will begin to reveal His true purpose for them when they embrace the principle of *"more of Him and less of me."*

Move Them Toward Ministry And Kingdom Business

Take them with you to church and conferences. We hold weekly intercessory prayer meetings in our home, and of course, our children are part of these sessions. We take them for evangelism and allow them to serve in our local family church in different ministries.

We take them to different provinces of Canada and the USA on outreaches and National Intercessory Conferences, and they willingly release and pray for me during my numerous ministry trips across the nations. I love hearing stories of how God has used them to share the gospel with their classmates and friends. Indeed, the fruit is worth waiting on God's time.

What The Bible Says About Christian Mothers

Being a mother is an important role that God gives to a woman. A Christian mother should love her children so that she does not bring reproach on the Lord and her Saviour (Titus 2:4).

To Love Her Children

Children are a gift from the Lord (Ps. 127:3-5). In Titus 2:4, the Greek word *philoteknos* appears in reference to mothers loving their children. This word represents a special kind of "mother love." A mother should care for her children, nurture them, affectionately embrace them, meet their needs and tenderly befriend each one as a unique gift from the hand of God. Several things commanded of Christian mothers in God's Word.

To be Available

> *These commandments that I give you today are to be on your hearts. Impress them on your children. Talk about them when you sit at home and when you walk along the road, when you lie down and when you get up.*

> **Deuteronomy 6:6-7**

To be Involved in the Affairs of the Children

Interact, discuss, think and process life together with your children *"Fathers, do not exasperate your children; instead, bring them up in the training and instruction of the Lord"* (Eph. 6:4).

To Teach the Children

> *He decreed statutes for Jacob and established the law in Israel, which he commanded our ancestors to teach their children, so the next generation would know them, even the children yet to be born, and they in turn would tell their children. Then, they would put their trust in God and would not forget his deeds but would keep his commands.*

> **Psalm 78:5-7**

Training the Children

A mother should help the child to develop skills and discover his or her strengths. Proverbs 22:6 says, *"Start children off on the way they should go, and even when they are old, they will not turn from it."*

Teach Them About
Spiritual Gifts

A spiritual gift is an extraordinary power given by the Holy Spirit, to a believer who receives salvation. These are the supernatural graces which individual Christians need to fulfill the mission of the Church. These "charismatic gifts" include word of wisdom, word of knowledge, increased faith, gifts of healing, gift of miracles, prophecy, discernment of spirits, diverse kinds of tongues, and interpretation of tongues.

Teaching The Fear Of The Lord And Drawing The Line Consistently, Lovingly But Firmly

> *And have you completely forgotten this word of encouragement that addresses you as a father addresses his son? It says, "My son, do not make light of the Lord's discipline, and do not lose heart when He rebukes you, because the Lord disciplines the one He loves, and He chastens everyone He accepts as His son." Endure hardship as discipline; God is treating you as his child. For what children are not disciplined by their father? If you are not disciplined—and everyone undergoes discipline—then you are not legitimate, not true sons and daughters at all. Moreover, we have all had*

human fathers who disciplined us, and we respected them for it. How much more should we submit to the Father of spirits and live! They disciplined us for a little while as they thought best; but God disciplines us for our good, in order that we may share in his holiness. No discipline seems pleasant at the time, but painful. Later on, however, it produces a harvest of righteousness and peace for those who have been trained by it.

Hebrews 12:5-11

Nurture

Nurture your children by giving them support and loving them affectionately and unconditionally. The Bible did not state that every woman should be a mother. However, it says that those whom the Lord blesses to be mothers should take the responsibility seriously. Mothers have a unique and crucial role to play in the lives of their children. Motherhood is not a chore or an unpleasant task. Just as a mother bears a child in her womb for nine months, a mother should care for her children from the infancy stage through the adolescence and youth stages. The love, care, nurture and encouragement that a mother gives to her children should never stop.

Chapter 12

FAITHFUL AND LOVING GOD

My godly seeds are my life's testimony of the reality of God. God is real. The knowledge of God is a supreme experience that is beyond doubt. I attended a traditional marriage ceremony of a relative. On my way, I told my cousin who was with me that I would find my wife there, even though I had not accepted Jesus Christ as my Lord and Saviour then. At the occasion, I saw Uche walking in with her friend. So, I got up and walked straight to her. I did not know how I got the boldness to approach her and even told her that she was my wife. She looked at me, said nothing, and walked past with her friend who happened to be a friend to my cousin.

The next year, we were invited to the Catholic Institute of West Africa (CIWA), Port Harcourt, for prayer of breaking family curses. I went with Uche to the program where I had the most wonderful experience of my life. I received Jesus Christ as my Lord and Saviour.

Uche and I started attending the discipleship training class with other youths and were very consistent in seeking spiritual insight and growth. There were weekly teachings on the *Gift of the Holy Spirit, Holy Ghost Baptism, the Fruits of the Holy Spirit* and *How to Discern the Right Spirit of God*. This group was also very prophetic as there were manifestations of the gifts of prophecy, word of knowledge, and word of wisdom according to the scripture. God said to us in one of the meetings that He shall establish our marriage and use it for His own glory. I froze where I was sitting. The same thing happened to Uche and we both prayed fervently. About a year later, we got married; our wedding was very prophetic and a fulfillment of God's Word.

Six months after our wedding, my employer sent me to the United Kingdom for a three-month management trainee program. During my stay in the UK, I had an encounter with the Lord who told me that He would be sending us out from Nigeria as missionaries to a foreign country. God also informed me that it would be in our mission field that we would have our children.

I told my wife about these revelations when I came back to Nigeria. She confirmed that she had prayed fervently for me while I was away. Three years later, the Lord revealed that He was sending us to Canada. Thereafter, I completed the immigration form to Canada and submitted it to the Canadian High Commission. In preparation, I resigned from my job with the hope of travelling within six months. Besides, we used the period to attend a school of missions and make preparations for the missionary work.

While waiting and seeking the face of the Lord for further direction, the Lord instructed me to start an HIV/AIDS rescue mission. So, with the Bible and the *Encyclopaedia of AIDS* given to me by one of our mentors, I began to research. When I was well equipped, the HIV/AIDS rescue mission work was registered as a Non-Governmental Organization under the Corporate Affairs Commission, Abuja, Nigeria.

We began the work of awareness, intervention, prevention and actual ministering to people infected with and affected by HIV. The results were remarkable, especially the number of people who accepted Jesus Christ as their personal Lord and Saviour through the rescue mission.

Although we were resident in Port Harcourt, the impact extended around Nigeria and the African continent. God began to open financial doors. Some HIV patients received divine

healing with medical laboratory test results to prove it. I was invited as one of the presenters at the Global Health Conference in Washington D.C. in May 2005. They were intrigued and wanted to know the best practice on how we achieved solutions to the HIV/AIDS pandemics in the sub-Saharan regions of Africa.

At the fullness of time, exactly our 10th marriage anniversary, we moved to Canada as missionary intercessors and Foreign Trained Professionals. During these years, my wife never had a missed period or miscarriage, so we were trusting God for the fruit of the womb, even though when we prayed for others, they conceived and gave birth to the glory of God.

In Canada, I reminded God of His promise that we would have our children in the mission field. I asked God to answer our prayer and to give us our children. We consulted a family doctor who referred us to a gynaecologist and an obstetrician who began their medical investigations and had us carry out various laboratory tests.

My test results showed that I had oligospermia, which refers to semen with a low concentration of sperm count. The results also showed a significant abnormality in sperm morphology and motility. He pointed out that most of them were dead cells. So, he referred me to a urologist.

On the part of my wife, the test result detected multiple uterine fibroids in the womb, but despite the doctors' report, we continued to pray and address the problems, now by their names. We prayed targeted and specific prayers against oligospermia, low sperm count, sperm morphology and motility problems; we prayed for the revival of dead cells.

We prayed that anointed sperm cells that defy all obstacles should be produced and empowered to fertilize the eggs. We continued to call the anointed seeds in terms of egg and sperm. We reminded our bodies that only one sperm out of the millions that are produced is required to do the job, so whether there is a low or high sperm count does not matter. Like Jonathan said, *"For nothing restrains the Lord from saving by many or by few"* (1 Sam. 14:6).

Jeremiah 32:27 says:

> *Behold, I am the Lord, the God of all flesh. Is there anything too hard for me?*

We started a twenty-one-day fasting and prayer program as directed by a trusted servant of the Most High God to intensify our prayer life. Initially, we prayed targeted prayers against the uterine fibroids. I specifically spoke to the womb to hear the Word of the Lord, that God created it to carry babies and not fibroids.

I commanded the uterine fibroids to wither and disappear from the space they are occupying illegally in the womb. I gave them automatic quit notice of twenty days to leave the womb and vanish. I commanded the uterine walls and their blood vessels to cut off blood supply to the fibroids in the name of Jesus Christ.

We prayed that all serpentine spirits that devour eggs and kill sperms be destroyed in the name of Jesus. During these twenty days, we continued fervently with the mission work. We reminded the Lord of His promise that we would have our children in our mission field.

Before the end of the twenty-one days' fasting and prayer, my wife felt a bit ill and we went to see the family doctor. On examination, the doctor decided to do a pregnancy test. The test result was positive for the first time ever. My wife was pregnant.

The appointment with the urologist came and we went. The urologist opened the file and explained the results. After the explanation, we informed the urologist that my wife was pregnant. He exclaimed with surprise, and said, "Oh, my job is done!"

The exploits of faith and life testimonies continued. Then our prayer focus changed. I laid my hands on and prayed for the baby in the womb every day and night. All my cuddling is to place my hand and pray for the baby in the womb. I daily commanded the baby to grow and that the fibroids should shrink and disappear in the name of Jesus. The ultrasound result showed that there were several uterine fibroids occupying the womb. According to the result, one of them measured about 13cm long. I told the baby that the womb belongs to her and that the baby should not share the space with any uterine fibroids.

At full gestation period, the baby was born. The baby weighed 10.8 pounds at birth. It was a supernatural birth and my godly seed. God is great; He answered our prayers and proved that He is faithful to His Word. May His name be glorified forever.

Fruitful Vine and Olive Shoots is our brief testimony. The Lord has blessed us with three Olive Shoots.

> *Your wife will be like a fruitful vine within your house; your children will be like olive shoots around your table.*

Psalm 128:3 NIV

Chapter 13

THE TESTIMONIES OF OUR OLIVE SHOOTS

My Glorious Life Journey

My name is Glory S. and I am thirteen years old, the eldest daughter of the Ezechim's family. I was told that I was a miracle baby. Naturally, being the oldest, I heard time and time again about my brother's and sister's birth testimonials, but as I'm growing older, I'm beginning to really understand its significance.

Recently, all was revealed about my mother conceiving me, so I'll share it with you in a nutshell. After waiting on God for a child for ten years, my parents finally started the process of childbearing by divine intervention.

My Dad, Ezekiel Ezechim was married to my Mom for about six months when he was sent to the United Kingdom from Nigeria as an Electrical Engineer with Michelin Nigeria Ltd, Port Harcourt. He sought the Lord for children and the Lord gave him a surprising answer: "*Your children will come when you move to the mission field*." After three months of working and pondering on the Lord's response, he was given another job offer. Still in the dark about the so-called 'mission field', my father brought this offer to God. God said that He had something better for dad. So, in obedience to God, my dad declined the offer to the surprise of the management of the company in the UK.

Thereafter, my Father returned to Nigeria and they continued to pray, love and serve the Lord wholeheartedly. He was reading a newspaper and saw an advertisement that was encouraging people to move to Canada, as Canada needed professionals. He knew that surely this was the plan of God, and my parents remembered what God said about having their children. They completed the applications and started the process. A few years later, they relocated to Canada where I was born in fulfillment of the promise of God to my parents.

How I Am Being Raised

I am being raised by my parents to be a positive role model; showing respect, responsibility, honour and consistency are some of my outstanding qualities. Apart from running our own ministry, my mom and dad have always encouraged me and my two siblings to read our Bibles and apply the truth of the Word of God in every aspect of our lives. I have personally read the Bible cover-to-cover three times. As the eldest of the three

children, I shall continue to model the fear and admonition of the Lord for my siblings.

Who I Am In Christ

I am very blessed. Life is a blessing as I am fearfully and wonderfully made. I am very thankful to God that I was born, and I try to make the most of each and every day. In Christ, I see myself as a daughter of Light, a minister in the making, a godly and righteous seed, waiting for her time to blossom and grow. I am part of a quickly-growing family, a branch that is about to spout and provide for many others.

I AM A COVENANT CHILD

My name is Covenant E. I am 12 years old and the second daughter of my parents, Uche and Ezekiel Ezechim.

My siblings are Glory and Jachimike. My favorite color is blue. I like to eat pizza and salad. I love going to the park. I hope to someday become a doctor and get a horse. I love animals. I play guitar and sometimes write songs when I practice. God enabled me to excel academically so I attend a special school for exceptionally gifted students.

I've heard the story of my birth countless times. I know that there were quite a few complications while I was in my mom's womb. I know that the devil tried not to allow me and my siblings to be born, but all his lies and tricks failed.

I am thankful for my life, and every day I always remember to thank God for life because every day is a blessing.

My parents raised me to always listen to them and to God. We go to church on Sundays and Wednesdays. I have gone to many conferences. We hold a lot of prayer meetings at home, in person, and on the phone. My parents taught me not to follow everything the world does because some of such things are ungodly. My parents have always taught me to be polite, obedient and to take care of my space. They teach me life lessons and always help with my homework. I love my parents a lot. I also love God very much. He is my best friend, my Lord, my Savior and He means so much to me. I like telling my friends about Jesus. I got one of my friends a Bible as her birthday gift and she was very happy. Every year, I try to read the whole Book and chapters of the Bible.

God With Jachimike

My name is Jachimike E. I am eight years old. I love to read the Bible, play soccer and play Lego. I love to watch films on Bible stories. I love my parents. I love the Lord very much with all my heart, soul, strength and might. My parents are teaching me to obey God and not to follow the earth. For example, if the whole world jumps off a cliff, a godly, wise person would not follow them because the person would likely die. I can see God telling me to keep going on my lifestyle. God bless you.

Echoes From The Family

When my sister asked me to write a few words on her book, *Fruitful Vine and Olive Shoots,* I became excited, and at the same time, anxious. I was excited because her story has been that of living by faith and not by sight, obedience to God's will, and a developed winner's mentality. I was anxious because I doubted I could possibly put in concrete terms what this woman of faith has passed through and how our family had perceived her journey of faith.

First, I thank God for the gift of our parents, and I remember our mother in a special way as I write this. Perhaps, she could have been the best person to write this if she were to be alive today. However, she is celebrated for praying fervently for her daughter, modeling her faith and training her up in the way she should go. Her prayers and tears have been heard by Our Lord Jesus Christ.

The title of this book is replete with meanings; Psalm 128:3 is a promise and blessing of God to those who fear God. The poet proves that everything depends upon the blessing of God. The building of the house, which affords us protection; the stability of the city in which we securely and peacefully dwell; the acquisition of possessions that maintain and adorn life; and the begetting and rearing of children that may contribute substantial support to the parents as they grow old, dependent upon the blessing of God without preliminary conditions to guarantee them.

I applaud the publication of your wonderful book on the manifestation of the divine inspiration and blessings of the Most High. It is a good reminder to look at the joyous side of our daily challenges. I have shared some of your stories with my friends and we have all found delight in them. Your story is a reference point for deeper faith, patience, and courage for our family. Your voice shall always be bright. Thank you for being a blessing and encouragement to us and to humanity. Thank you for sharing with us the gift that you have worked so hard to refine. Indeed, you are a fruitful vine and your children are true olive shoots. May your childbearing journey continue to be a testimony for those who trust the Lord God Almighty.

Very Rev. Dr. George N. Okeahialam, MSP
Regional Superior, Missionary Society of St. Paul American
Region Houston, Texas

Praise Report

By Mrs. Ngozi Adiuku
Orangeville, Canada

Thank you for the opportunity to share my testimony. I have tried to make it as brief as possible. Please feel free to revise as needed. May this book bless couples all around the world and open up wombs to the glory of God.

Praise be to God Almighty for His unfailing love towards us. My twins were born when I was thirty-six years old after waiting on God for several years. Two years after the twins, I was ready to have another child and trusted that God would again come through for me. I had about two cycles of IVF treatment in the United States that were unfruitful. On relocating to Canada, I tried the IVF treatment again without any success. In fact, I was given expired drugs during one of those cycles, which I never realized until the cycle failed.

Sister Uche and I prayed for supernatural childbirth; she would call me every Saturday with some powerful prayer points which I wrote down as quickly as I could. God heard our prayers as I connected to the grace that was upon her life. She did not just pray for me but was a big source of encouragement as well. One of the days during my pregnancy, she called me while I was at work and said that I was not happy. Truly, at that time, I was on my way to the sick room because I was not feeling too well. I was amazed that she called me at that moment and that God had revealed how I was feeling at that time to her. She encouraged and prayed for me. She was a source of physical and spiritual support all through the duration of the pregnancy and afterward. The rest of my pregnancy was trouble-free and I saw myself glowing in the glory of God with each passing day.

The prayers were so powerful that my colleague knew whenever I was praying; he would turn around and ask me if I had started praying those prayers again. I was amazed because this guy was not a Christian and I wondered how he knew that I was praying even though my lips were not moving.

Eventually, we got talking and I found out that he and his wife were seeking for the fruit of the womb. I started to pray for him without his knowledge and offered him a copy of the prayer points, not knowing whether he would accept it or not.

He was very hesitant to accept it from me and I eventually told him there was no harm in leaving it at his desk and he could resort to

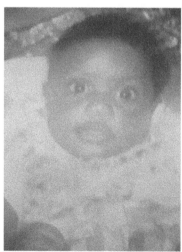

it if he changed his mind. To the glory of God, before I left for my maternity leave, he gave the good news that his wife had conceived, and I later learned that they had a baby girl.

My testimony begat a testimony. Someone once said that where we take our problems will determine the outcome. Our God is indeed a solution provider and a miracle worker Who brought about the conception and birth of baby Praise after ten years. In spite of the challenges of age, which the doctors never ceased to throw in my face, God came through for me. At forty-six years, I had baby Praise to the glory of God without complications nor birth defects as speculated by the doctors. To God be the glory!

Chapter 14

SUPERNATURAL CONCEPTION AND DIVINE PROTECTION PROGRAM

This program is for people who have the following issues:

- Repeated miscarriage
- Difficulty in conceiving a child
- Damaged or removed reproductive organs or womb
- Classified impotency
- Low sperm count
- Uterine fibroids
- Bloated fallopian tubes
- Curses and evil covenants

Secrets To Success

1. **Husbands and wives should actively participate in this program.** *Again, I say to you that if two of you agree on earth concerning anything that they ask, it will be done for them by My Father in heaven* (Matt. 18:19).

2. **Follow the outlined steps provided in this book to organize your own personal deliverance.** Say the Lord's Prayer that, *God would not lead us into temptation but deliver us*

from the evil one. For yours is the kingdom and the power and the glory forever. Amen (Matt. 6:13).

3. **Seek prayer of healing and deliverance from other believers and the elders of the church.** *Is anyone among you sick? Let him call for the elders of the church, and let them pray over him, anointing him with oil in the name of the Lord* (James 5:14).

4. **Endeavour to seek help from and rely on the Holy Spirit, who knows your specific needs more than anyone.** *But if I cast out demons with the finger of God, (with the Holy Spirit), surely the kingdom of God has come upon you* (Luke 11:20).

5. **Get rid of negative feelings and emotions, such as anger, anxiety, agitation, depression, bitterness, feelings of frustration and shame.** The Bible admonishes us to; *Cease from anger and forsake wrath; do not fret – it only causes harm* (Eph. 4:31). *Be anxious for nothing, but in everything by prayer and supplication, with thanksgiving, let your requests be made known to God* (Phil. 4:6).

6. **Know and believe that there is nothing impossible for God to do.** Luke 1:37 says, *For with God nothing will be impossible.*

7. **Understand that the report of God is superior to the report of all doctors, specialists and consultants.** Lamentations 3:37 says, *Who is he who speaks, and it comes to pass, When the Lord has not commanded it?*

8. **Give God quality praise and worship before praying each day.** *God is Spirit, and those who worship Him must worship in spirit and truth* (John 4:24).

9. **Forgive your offenders and yourself of past mistakes.** *For if you forgive other people when they sin against you, your heavenly Father will also forgive you. But if you do*

not forgive others their sins, your Father will not forgive your sins (Matt. 6:14-15).

10. **Create time to pray and have vigil.** Matthew 26:40 says, *"Then he returned to his disciples and found them sleeping." "Couldn't you men keep watch with me for one hour?" he asked Peter. "So, Watch and pray so that you will not fall into temptation. The spirit is willing, but the flesh is weak"* (Mark 14:38).

11. **Anoint your reproductive organs such as your lower abdomen and underneath the belly before or after praying.***They drove out many demons and anointed many sick people with oil and healed them* (Mark 6:13).

12. **Respect the peace of your homes.** Let your home be a place of rest for you and your spouse. Deal with the spirit of nagging, strife, argument and debate (Ps. 37:8). *Let all bitterness, wrath, anger, clamor, and evil speaking be put away from you, with all malice.*

13. **Be spiritually open or naked to each other.** Confess your sins to one another, particularly, sexual sins.*Therefore, confess your sins to each other and pray for each other so that you may be healed...* (James 5:16a).

14. **Speak faith language to each other by declaring the Word of God loud and clear to that situation.** *Then the Lord reached out his hand and touched my mouth and said to me, "I have put my words in your mouth. See, today I appoint you over nations and kingdoms to uproot and tear down, to destroy and overthrow, to build and to plant* (Jer. 1:9-10).

Then he said to me, "Prophesy to the breath; prophesy, son of man, and say to it, 'this is what the Sovereign Lord says: Come, breathe, from the four winds and breathe into these slain, that they may live.'

Ezekiel 37:9

Forty Prophetic Breakthrough Prayer Points

1. My brothers and sisters, *put on the whole armor of God, that you may be able to stand against the wiles of the devil and that you may be able to withstand in the evil day, and having done all, to stand (Eph. 6:11).*
   - ❖ Gird your waist with the belt of truth
   - ❖ Wear the breastplate of righteousness over your chest-Shod your feet with the sandals of the gospel of peace
   - ❖ Carry the shield of faith on your left hand with which you will quench all the fiery darts of the wicked one
   - ❖ Cover your head with the helmet of salvation
   - ❖ Carry the sword of the Spirit on your right hand; that is the Word of God
   - ❖ Open your mouth to pray always; let your request and supplication be known to God through the help of the Holy Spirit
   - ❖ Watch with all perseverance; be sober, be vigilant because your adversary the devil is walking about like a roaring lion, seeking whom he may devour.
2. O Lord, dig to the foundation of my problems by fire, in the name of Jesus.
3. Whatever my heavenly Father has not planted in my womb be destroyed by the blood of Jesus, in the name of Jesus.
4. Every serpent that eats sperms and devours the eggs in the womb roast by the fire of the Holy Spirit, in Jesus name.

5. I retrieve all my personal belongings from the camp of the wicked that are being used to manipulate my life and marriage, in the name of Jesus.

6. O Lord, let Your Word become flesh in my life and replace every damaged cell and organ in my body, in the name of Jesus.

7. I prophesy that all my reproductive systems are in perfect condition, in Jesus' name.

8. I reject, revoke, annul and reverse every curse of infertility, barrenness and unfruitfulness in my life and marriage, in the name of Jesus.

9. I evacuate by fire and the blood of Jesus, every evil deposit in my womb, in the name of Jesus.

10. I break every covenant of infertility through sex, abortions and incisions in my life, in the name of Jesus.

11. I purge and flush my womb and other reproductive organs with the blood of Jesus in the name of Jesus.

12. The Bible says that God sent His word and healed them, and delivered them from their destructions. Therefore, I command healing and restoration to any damaged or malfunctioning cell, tissue, tube and organ, in the name of Jesus.

13. I loose my womb and reproductive organs from every witchcraft spell, jinx, voodoo and enchantment, in the name of Jesus.

14. Let the fire of God melt and consume every evil padlock, chain and cord used to tie my womb, in the name of Jesus.

15. O Lord, arise and send fire to destroy all evil altars and priests sitting upon my womb and marriage in the name of Jesus.

16. I praise God that I am fearfully and wonderfully made: therefore, I cannot be barren, in the name of Jesus.

17. I pray and command all my children to come forth to me now, in the name of Jesus.

18. My Father and my Lord, please take away every shame, reproach, confusion and frustration from my life and family, in the name of Jesus.

19. Holy Ghost, please turn my sorrows to happiness, my disappointments to divine appointments, my failure to success, and my pains to gains, in Jesus' name.

20. I declare that I will carry my baby without miscarriage or still-birth; I will not labor in vain and I will not die at childbirth, in the name of Jesus.

21. I renounce and cancel with the blood of Jesus, every evil blood covenant entered into by me, my parents or my ancestors, in the name of Jesus.

22. I repent of any promise I made, consciously or unconsciously, to the kingdoms of darkness using my future children, in the name of Jesus.

23. I break and destroy every spiritual marriage covenant in my life, in Jesus' name.

24. I vomit out and expunge every contamination through food, drink, sex and drugs, in the dream, in Jesus' name.

25. I eliminate and wash from my organs any pollution, disease, infirmity and damage caused through sexual immorality, in the name of Jesus.

26. I terminate any contracts I have with the spirits of barrenness and miscarriage, in the name of Jesus.

27. O God, burn and destroy the agents of darkness and their instruments used in monitoring me, in the name of Jesus.

28. I bless the Lord, who forgives all my iniquities, who heals all my diseases, who redeems my life from destruction, who crowns me with lovingkindness and tender mercies.

29. Bless me, O God, beyond measure with my godly and anointed children, in the name of Jesus.

30. Every power that is working against the manifestation of my miracle children in the heavenlies, on the earth, underneath

the earth, in the water, and from the outer space, I command you to bow down in Jesus' name.

31. Father, send godly doctors, nurses, midwives, pharmacists, medical laboratory specialists and other medics to me in Jesus' name.

32. Father Lord, please frustrate the tokens of the liars and make the diviners run mad, in Jesus' name.

33. Oh! God that answered Hannah, Elizabeth, and Sarah, please answer me also in Jesus' name.

34. I command every blessing confiscated by familiar or ancestral spirits and my enemies, to be released in the name of Jesus.

35. May every evil altar where my name has been mentioned for evil be destroyed, in the name of Jesus.

36. Let every tree and pot planted over my umbilical cord or foreskin be rooted out, in the name of Jesus.

37. Children are the heritage of the Lord and the fruit of the womb is His reward. Therefore, everything contesting against my children must die, in the name of Jesus.

38. Let every dead organ in my life receive life now, in the name of Jesus.

39. I curse and break the power of impotence and low sperm count in my life, in the name of Jesus.

40. I command every manipulation of darkness over my manhood to be destroyed, in the name of Jesus.

BIBLIOGRAPHY

Abate, Matthew J. "A Fruitful Vine and Olive Shoots." MatthewJAbate.wordpress.com. Accessed December 28, 2019. https://matthewjabate.wordpress.com/2014/03/18/a-fruitful-vine-and-olive-shoots/.

CBN.com. "What Is Intercessory Prayer?" CBN.com. Accessed December 29, 2019. http://www1.cbn.com/questions/what-is-intercessory-prayer.

Conner, Polly and Tiemeyer, Rachel. "Where is God When You Can't Get Pregnant." Thrivinghomeblog.com. Accessed December 28, 2019. https://thrivinghomeblog.com/2015/03/where-is-god-when-you-cant-get-pregnant/.

Curtis, Mike, "5 'Stones' Needed to Raise World Changers." Charismamag.com. Accessed November 30, 2018. https://www.charismamag.com/life/family-parenting/23576-5-stones-needed-to-raise-world-changers.

De Lashmut, Garyt. "Increasing Your Capacity to Receive God's Love." XENOS Christian Fellowship, xenos.org. Accessed December 28, 2019 https://www.xenos.org/teachings/?teaching=1029.

Eze-Uzomaka, Pamela. *Holy Spirit My Best Friend*. CreateSpace Independent Publishing Platform, October 12, 2013.

Hodge, Meredith. " Have You Ocercome Infertility Or Are You Overcome by It?" Meredith Hodge Blog. Accessed November 30, 2018.

http://itspositiveliving.com/overcome-infertility/

Institute in Basic Life Principles. "What Does It Mean to 'Stand Alone'?" IBLP.org. Accessed December 28, 2019. https://iblp. org/questions/what-does-it-mean-stand-alone.

LaHaye, Beverly,. *The New Spirit-Controlled Woman*. Harvest House Publishers; revised edition July 1, 2005.

Le Claire, Jennifer. "5 Reasons You Really Need More Holy Ghost"

Charismamag.com. Accessed December 28, 2019. https://www. charismamag.com/blogs/the-plumb-line/26288-5-reasons-you-really-need-more-holy-ghost.

Macarthur, John. "What Kind of Things Do and Do Not Prove the Genuineness of Saving Faith?" GTY.org. Accessed December 28, 2019. https://www.gty.org/library/questions/QA145/ what-kind-of-things-do-and/-do-not-prove-the-genuiness-of-saving faith.

Medical News Today. "Infertility in Men and Women." Medicalnewstoday.com. Accessed November 30, 2018. http:// www.medicalnewstoday.com/articles/165748.php.

Mize, Jackie. *Supernatural Childbirth*. Harrison House, July 1, 1993.

Nordquist, Christian (2018) *Infertility in Men and Women* Reviewed by Debra Rose Wilson, PhD, MSN, RN, IBCLC, AHN-

BC, CHT.

Ogan, Steve. *How to Beat Your In-Laws*. Uzima Press, 2001.

Olukoya, D. K. (2016) *Deliverance God's Medicine Bottle*. The Battle Cry Christian Ministries, July 30, 2014.

Omartian, Stormie , "God's Divine Destiny: Laying Hold of Your Purpose." Charismamag.com. Accessed November 30, 2018.

https://www.charismamag.com/site-archives/610-spirit-led-woman/spiritled-woman/7215-gods-divine-destiny-laying-hold-of-your-purpose.

Oregondoula.com. "A Fruitful Vine." Oregondoula.com. Accessed December 28, 2019.http://www.oregondoula.com/Zion/A_fruitful_vine.htm

Robins, Dale A. "The Power of Praise & Worship." The Victorious Network, victorious.org. http://www.victorious.org/pub/praise-worship-123.

Stanley, Charles. *Charles Stanley's Handbook for Christian Living: Biblical Answers to Life's Tough Questions*. Thomas Nelson, October 14, 2008.

Williams, John and Kay. "Deliverance." Totallifeministries.org .Accessed December 28, 2019. http://www.totallifeministries.org/Articles/Deliverance.htm.

Wohl, Candace (2015) *Our Misconceptions. (This is a blog, dated October 25, 2017 Celeste's story) Accessed November 30, 2018. https://www.ourmisconception.com/*

AGC Scholarships. "Surviving Infertility in a Fertile World on Mother's Day." ACGscolarships.org. Accessed November 30, 2018. https://agcscholarships.org/surviving-mothers-day

worldometers. http://www.worldometers.info/abortions/.

Medical News Today. "Infertility In Men and Women." Medicalnewstoday.com. Accessed November 30, 2018. http://www.medicalnewstoday.com/articles/165748.php.

Lightning Source UK Ltd.
Milton Keynes UK
UKHW020747250420
362243UK00018B/1592